中國夢‧廣東故事
——共享的廣東

作者　王鶴　WANG HE

The China Dream : Guangdong Story - Common Prosperity

Editors: Wang Ning, Shi Yong

Published by Guangdong People's Publishing House Ltd., China

www.gdpph.com

First published 2017

Printed in the People's Republic of China

The China Dream: Guangdong Story- Common Prosperity/ Wang He and translated by Jin Yang

ISBN 978-7-218-11892-5 (paperback, 1st edition)

Preface

Located in southern China, Guangdong Province is the first region in China to implement the reform and opening up, and it is also one of the most affluent areas nationwide. The Pearl River, China's third largest river, runs across the whole province. The Pearl River Delta is an alluvial plain flushed by the Pearl River. After nearly 40 years of rapid development, it has already become one of the most important city groups of China. The Hong Kong Special Administrative Region, and the Macao Special Administrative Region adjoin to Guangdong Province. With the natural geographical relations and the same cultural background, they constitute China's unique Guangdong-Hong Kong-Macao Greater Bay Area—a world-class vigorous economic and cultural area.

For nearly 40 years of rapid development, Guangdong has been playing a leading role in innovation, spurring the rapid development of new growth drivers. There are many rapidly grown-up enterprises in Guangdong, such as Huawei, Tencent, and UMi, which have become important engines of Guangdong's new economy development. Huawei and Tencent are now widely known in China. We try to approach such enterprises and their employees, to find the "secret" of the most innovative and cutting-edge development in Guangdong.

Guangdong has been the most dynamic foreign trade area in China since ancient times. And Guangzhou has been a commercial city through the ages, as well as an important interconnecting city alongside the "Maritime Silk Road". Foreigners from all over the world travel across major cities in Guangdong everyday, sightseeing, attending business meetings, studying or visiting friends. In Guangzhou, there are a large number of foreigners from Europe, America, Southeast Asia, the Middle East, Africa and other places, doing business here everyday. They ship back clothing, fabric, seafood, electrical appliances or glasses; foreign trade is booming. In the Shenzhen Special Economic Zone ports, people and vehicles travelling between Hong Kong and Shenzhen are always lined up. Foreigners living here for many years gradually adopt and merge into customs and culture of Guangdong, and regard Guangdong as their "second home". Meanwhile, tens of millions of workers from other provinces live in Guangdong, especially in the Pearl River Delta, where they work in factories, earn money to support their families, and try to realize their own dreams and ambitions. Whether foreigners or migrant workers, they are all practitioners, promoters and witnesses of Guangdong's reform and opening up. We conduct close observation of their work and life to record their ups and downs.

Ten years ago, the per capita income in the Pearl River Delta had already reached the level of that of moderately developed countries, and it is moving towards high-income phase. But the embarrassment is that in the eastern, western and northern parts of Guangdong Province, there are still large number of underdeveloped rural areas, and some places are even in extreme poverty, which distresses successive provincial governments. The government is determined to carry out large-scale " poverty alleviation" action, and vows to lift all peasants of impoverished areas out of poverty in three years, and promote common prosperity in these parts of Guangdong like the Pearl River Delta.

As the most populated, dynamic, and developed province that has been spearheading reform and opening up, recent practices in Guangdong are full of strength and sweetness. We go into it, and hope to find and record those breathtaking, touching and impressive stories of the development in Guangdong these years. Those people and those stories constitute a glaring part in the glittering development of the new era in Guangdong.

Through these stories, you can see diligence and endeavors of Guangdong people in the process of modernization. Through the perspective of Guangdong, you can see great efforts of Chinese people in realizing the China dream of the great rejuvenation of the Chinese nation.

總序

　　廣東省位於中國南部，是中國最早實行改革開放的區域，也是目前中國最富庶的地區之一。中國的第三大河流珠江穿越廣東省全境，由珠江沖積而成的珠江三角洲在經過近四十年迅速發展後，已經成為中國最重要的城市群之一。香港特別行政區、澳門特別行政區與廣東省毗鄰，天然的地緣和一脈相承的人文情緣，構成了中國獨有的粵港澳大灣區——一個世界級活躍的經濟人文區域。

　　和中國其他地區一樣，在經過長達近四十年的高速發展之後，廣東面臨產業轉型升級轉變發展動能的重任，創新驅動成為推動此輪變革的重要抓手。廣東省內有許多近年來快速成長起來的新型企業，比如華為、騰訊、有米科技，它們成為廣東新經濟發展的重要引擎。華為和騰訊，以及它們的「老闆」任正非和馬化騰，在中國幾乎家喻戶曉。我們試圖走近這樣的企業及其員工，找到廣東創新驅動最前沿的發展「密碼」。

　　廣東自古以來是中國對外商貿最活躍的地區，廣州是千年商都，是「海上絲綢之路」重要的節點城市。來自世界各地的外國人每天往來於廣東省內各大城市，他們或旅遊觀光，或商務會議，或求學訪友。在廣州，每天大量來自歐美、東南亞、中東和非洲等地的外國人在這裡做生意，他們把這裡的服裝、布匹、海產品、電器或者眼鏡託運回國，外貿做得紅紅火火。在深圳經濟特區口岸，進出香港和深圳的車輛、人流常常排成長龍。長年生活在這裡的外國人，在生活習俗和文化上逐漸接受並慢慢融入廣東，廣東成為他們的「第二故鄉」。與此同時，更多的數千萬計的來自中國內地的普通勞工常年生活在廣東尤其是珠江三角洲地區，他們在工廠裡「打工」，憑藉「打工」掙下的錢養家餬口，並試圖實現自己的人生夢想。無論是外國人還是農民工，他們都是廣東改革開放的實踐者、推動者和見證者。我們近距離觀察他們的工作和生活，記錄他們的喜怒哀樂。

珠江三角洲地區早在十年前人均收入便已達到中等發達國家水平，正邁向高收入階段。但令人尷尬的是，在廣東省的東、西、北部仍有大片生活並不富裕的農村，一些地方甚至還處於貧困狀態，這讓廣東省歷屆政府頗感頭痛。政府下決心開展大規模的「扶貧」行動，並發誓要在三年後讓所有貧困地區的農民擺脫貧困，力促粵東西北地區與珠江三角洲地區走向共同富裕。

作為人口最多、經濟最活躍、總量最大、地處改革開放前沿的省份，廣東近年的實踐既具有力量又讓人感到溫馨。我們深入其中，希望通過我們去發現去記錄，在廣東發展這些年中，那些或動人心魄或充滿溫情或飽含人性的故事。那些人，那些事，終將構成廣東新時期史詩般發展歷程中炫目的一環。

通過這些故事，人們可以看見，在現代化進程中廣東人的奮發圖景；透過廣東，可以看見中國人民為實現中華民族偉大復興的中國夢的奮鬥歷程。

Contents

Establishing Transportation System to Relieve Poverty: Building a Good Road for Villages——A Way Out and A Way to Survive

Financial Poverty Alleviation: Stepping up the Way of Overcoming Poverty

Technology Accelerates Poverty Alleviation

High-speed Railways Have Changed the Lifestyles in Mountain Areas

Characteristic Towns: It's Nice Living in Mountain Villages

目錄

Poverty Alleviation of Guangdong's Poorest Villages: Eradicating Poverty in Limestone Mountain Regions

Leftovers in the Limestone Regions

In the movie *The Martian*, the hero Matt Monda, who is stuck on Mars alone and plants potatoes to live on, faces extremely difficult conditions. But at least the soil is fertile and he can harvest potatoes season after season. In Mengshan Village, however, with sufficient air, arable land and water are rare.

The limestone regions in Guangdong are 6,208 sq. km., accounting for 3.5% of the total area in the province and are mainly located in the northern and western part, with a few in the northeast. These regions share one thing in common: most of Guangdong's poorest villages are in these regions.

Mengshan is a small village located in Libu Town, Yangshan County of the northern Guangdong. It is a typical limestone region, with severe lack of soil and water, and an average attitude of over 500 meters. According to a survey conducted by the residency poverty-alleviation group when they first came to the village seven years ago, among all the 378 households were 127 poor families (437 people) and 69 families (171 people) with minimum allowances.

Why is Mengshan such a poor village? Let us first look at its natural environment conditions. In a mountain area, the most precious thing for farmers is arable land. However, all the land in Mengshan is scattered on the limestone hillside and, the small patches of land could hardly yield any economic benefits. Therefore, Mengshan villagers have to live toughly in the fragility of natural economy for the lack of mines, factories and power to change nature.

Many locals find it hard to describe their own farmland with exact words. The most classic self-mocking joke here is that on a rainy day, a farmer went up the mountain to cultivate land wearing a bamboo hat and when he arrived, the rain had stopped so he threw away the hat on the ground and started to turn the soil piece by piece. But after a day's exhausting work, he found that there was a missing patch of his land. He gave up looking for it and was about to pack things and went back home at dusk when he suddenly found the missing patch of land as he picked up the hat and discovered under it. This joke may sound exaggerated, but it shows exactly the embarrassing situation the villagers have been facing.

The scattering patches of land make it impossible to apply intensive farming in limestone areas. And even there are some plantable fields, the variety of crops is limited. High-value crops can barely be cultivated and only those like cassava and corn can grow in these fields.

The harsh environment also results in a drastic shortage of infrastructure construction. 285 out of the 440 units of paddy fields in Mengshan village are "fields on hill tops which depend on rains for irrigation" . Chen Jinsheng, head of the village committee, once said: "We can only harvest once a year and are not able to have irrigated agriculture. It's like watching the rain falls and having no way to keep and utilize it."

Long before the poverty alleviation group came, villagers had dreamed

The China Dream:Guangdong Story, *common Prosperity* of digging several ponds to ease the lack of agricultural irrigation and drinking water. As early as the beginning of the 21st century, the locals have excavated a rill in the mountains which funnels the mountain spring water. Due to the financial limitations, the water was first funnelled into some 2-meter deep impounding reservoirs and when villagers used pipes to pump the water to their own house, there was little left.

Digging ponds and wells was the only way to solve the whole village's drinking water problem and the investment for this was up to RMB 200,000. But it was embarrassing that back then the village's income relied mainly on migrant workers' income and earnings from planting corps such as tea-oil trees and the average annual income per person could barely reached RMB 3,000, so it was totally impossible for them to spare money to build water conservancy project when they could hardly cover their daily expenses.

With global warming and stronger El Nino phenomenon, the World Bank has warned that 100 million people would become poor due to climate changes. And villagers from high-attitude limestone mountain areas in Guangdong are among this group.

Those living in limestone areas depend on Heaven for food, and once they encounter natural disasters like storms, snows, droughts and floods, they become even more vulnerable. Villagers with capability and skills have left the place for a better life. By 2013, no new house had been built in

Mengshan Village and most of the local residents lived in the adobe house built between the 1930s and 1950s, with 1960s' slogans left on the exterior walls.

A Hometown
Migrants Cannot Go Back to

In 2016, China's "floating population" has reached 245,000,000. The phrase "floating population" refers to those who leave their domiciles of origin and live in other parts of China. In nearly 40 years after China's reform and opening up, the domestic floating population has been increasing, with a drastic growth after the 1990s, which went up from 6,570,000 in 1982 to 220,000,000 in 2010. It now accounts for 17% of the total population. In cities like Beijing, Shanghai and Guangzhou, the floating population occupies 40% of the local inhabitants. And most of them are young labor force moving from rural areas to cities.

The floating population go to big cities for better job opportunities and better lives. Seven years ago, most of the villages in the mountainous regions were bleak and desolate. Most of the villagers had left, leaving the elderly and children or those who had to take care of the elderly behind.

Has there been any changes in these villages in the past decade? The answer is yes. Actually some changes did take place in Mengshan village. But for the recent ten years, the only changes in most villagers' eyes lie in the construction of a gravel road and a two- storey committee office building. In 1997, the villagers raised about 20,000 yuan to construct a path toward bamboo forest and ponds. And the office building constructed in 1999 was sponsored by outworkers of Mengshan registry and poverty alleviation groups paid off the debts of the building construction.

Under the dual pressure of barren geographical conditions and gradually frequent natural disasters, some competent villagers chose to make a breakthrough for their lives by migrating and floating. But it didn't go smoothly. They lacked the skills and techniques to let them settle and develop in a new environment. They also faced a series of social problems such as children's education, employment and birth control planning due to the registry of residence.

In the 1990s, villagers made their first group leave to pull down buildings in Shunde, Foshan. However, most of the able-bodied men returned to the village because they earned little money and could not get accustomed to the lives outside the mountains. Xiong Huolan, a 67-year-old man took a different path. Instead of serving as a buildingdismantling worker, he made his living on picking up rubbish in Lianzhou, a nearby county-level city. The work of Xiong is similar to that of those in Brazil slums. At that time China's main cities didn't set up a garbage classification system, and these junkmen took back the whole city's rubbish and picked out the recyclable materials to sell for the second time, which realized the full utilization of these materials. By virtue of his diligence and perseverance, Xiong got married when he was in his fifties. In Mengshan, the number of villagers like Xiong, who migrated to other places to make a living, has increased gradually in the first decade of the 21st century. In December 2000, the population in Mengshan was 1,944 and by the end of 2009 it had dropped to 1,823, apart from the few deceased people, the deducted population was mostly migrants.

But migration is not a once-for-all thing. For those migrants, they still face problems when they are making the transitions from countrymen to urbanites and it is not easy for them to have a durable and stable development because most of them have no specific skills.

▲ In Lianma Village, Conghua, most of the young people have moved to cities or towns and just a few scattered households are living here.

Poverty Alleviation: Giving Hope to the Stay-at-home

The poverty of limestone mountain areas has long been a dilemma for Guangdong poverty alleviation work. For an area like Mengshan village, its deficiency in production resources and harsh living conditions dampens the effectiveness of government unremitting efforts in undertaking development-oriented antipoverty measures.

From 1997, the local government did a series of work to help the poor in the area, such as distributing farming funds in order to help farmers invest enough money for production. But because of the difficulties in technology and sales, most of these farming funds became "living funds" and thus failed to reverse the impoverished living conditions.

How to vitalize local economy is really much learning. Mengshan village has a new look now: lush camellia trees are all over the mountains, sparkling white flowers give off light fragrance... Starting from the beginning of 2009, Guangdong Power Grid Qingyuan Administration of Power Supply and Yangshan Supply and Marketing Cooperative worked hand in hand with Mengshan, Libu Town to adopt aiding measures. In three years' time, the 127 poverty-stricken households in the village have basically got rid of poverty.

The locals did a thorough survey on the prospects of camellia and found that if 120 trees were planted in one unit of land and every unit produced 200 jin of tea oil, then they could got an overall income of 4,000 yuan at the average price of 20 yuan/jin. Currently there are around 400 units of land in Mengshan and each poor household could be allocated a plantation area from 2 to 5 units respectively.

It usually requires 3 to 5 years for a tea oil tree to produce fruits and about 10 years to reach the period of full productive years, with a steady fruit-harvest time for more than 80 years. Zhu Caiying, a 54 years old man is the only working labor in the family after his adult son developed mental disorder. His wife passed away due to cancer 8 years ago and they spent all the 100,000 savings for her treatment. Zhu said that: "I lent the 2 units of land to those who plant camellia trees and I'm also working for them. So as more fruits are harvested, I can earn more money in the future."

Financial Measures Taken to Help the Poorest Villages

The assistance group brought about production poverty elimination and also financial poverty relief. Yangshan was the first to put forward the idea of "poverty relief managers" and designated as "managers" village leaders or competent people who would work voluntarily to help the poor households. Residential village leaders looked for poor people who are diligent and have a strong desire to get rid of poverty, and helped them hand in hand. Yangshan Poverty Relief Office enlarged production by lending money to support "managers" and helped the poor through the efforts of those "managers".

What is more important is that Yangshan Poverty Relief Office underwrites 100,000 yuan for every village in the bank for a permission of 500,000 loans and has the "managers" act as underwriters. Supported by such financial innovation, Mengshan equips itself with several large-scale farming bases.

Villagers have long been facing the problem of fund shortage. To help Menghan raise enough funding, assistance group made a creative move of setting up the village-level mutual help funds.

"Such funds can be view as 'village-level banks' ", introduced by Pan Zhiwei, director of Poverty Relief and Development Office. Village-

▲ On the morning of 30 June, 2016, the 2016 Guangdong Poverty Relief Day was launched in Guangzhou Zhudao Hotel. The charitable representatives from Guangdong enterprises and warm-hearted people attended the meeting and made donations. Guangdong Poverty Relief Outstanding Team (Project) raised banners to introduce the public charity projects.

level assistance funds are mainly raised by the government and nearly 400,000 yuan has been raised for Mengshan. The poor can lend 3,000 yuan with depositing any money in the bank.

"If working with a leading enterprise, we can apply loan that is no more than five-fold of the assistance fund from the agricultural bank." Pan elaborated this with an example, one poor household can apply 45,000 yuan loans from the agricultural bank if it can borrow 9,000 yuan at most.

Of course, the poor cannot casually borrow money from village assistance organizations unless they are underwritten by rich and influential families or more than three households. The "village-level banks" arouse villagers' interest in development. A villager called Jiang Siwen told us it cost 100,000 yuan to build a hog house to feed 300 pigs. Depending solely on himself, he could hardly raise so much money. But with the help of village-level mutual help funds, he finally made it to get tens of thousands of yuan. He said: "My ultimate goal is to have a hog house which can afford to feed housands of pigs."

Getting Rid of Poverty: Gaining Better Livelihood through Integral Moving

Considering the special geological features of limestone area and harsh living and production conditions, the locals in the mountainous areas in northern Guangdong have been alleviating poverty by effectively relocating people for the past decade. A relatively mature model for the locals is to move migrant population to a specific area and help them solve the problems of employment and children's education. It turns out that after the relocation, the residents have a higher income and mostly merges into the re-settlement communities.

Zhongchong is a village in Daqiao Town, Ruyuan Yao Autonomous County of Shaoguan, which is located deep in mountains and in the past, if one wants to get into the village, he would have to travel through highway to national road then to rural road and lanes.

It is one of the few villages in Guangdong that snow in winter and the mountains are covered in yellow when November comes every year. This place is a sleeping country compared with the Pearl River Delta though it lies in the south of the Five Ridges.

However, things have changed. The Yao New Village on the hillside was built by the migrant Zhongchong villagers. Moving from mountains to the edge of the county, they now have a three-mile distance to the county and have a convenient transport because there is a newly-built round-the mountain-road at the gate of the village.

The relocation changes people's travel habits. For example, if the villager Zhao Tianxiang wants to go to the town before the 2010, he would leave his house at dawn, walk for four hours on the mountain roads and rushed back home after quickly buying all the necessities in the county. This is because the route would get dangerous after it gets dark due to the narrow roads and steep cliffs.

▲ In 9 August, 2011, the major parts of the first stage of Liwan-Lutian counterpart-assistance project have been completed and Su Zhijia dedicated the project. The project started from 18 May and was completed 20 days ahead of the planning date. The photo is the completion of the project's major parts. Photo taken by Gu Zhanxu.

After the reconstruction of Zhongchong village, children can study in the county's primary schools. The New Village is built in the style of Yao Minority and every villager has a two-storey building which has white walls, green bricks and red handrails, painted with Yao's ancient ornamentations. Leaving the mountains, villagers have more choices to make a living, such as engaging in agriculture or working in various industries.

Zhongchong started high mountain vegetable plantation from 2010 and now there are three bases: vegetable base, camellia base and yellow smoke base. High mountain vegetable has become a brand in Guangdong, and with eggplants, peppers and green beans transported to places like Guangzhou, Shenzhen, Dongguan, Daqiao Town (the place where Zhongchong is located) has become the vegetable basket in the Pearl River Delta.

Zhongchong is just an epitome of the integral moving in Guangdong poor mountainous areas. Dating back to the 1990s, Guangdong has begun the enormous work of migrant relocation. 100,000 Qingyuan Villagers have realized resettlement between 1994 and 1997 and another 300,000 Guangdong poor villagers made it from 2011 to 2016. After the relocation, the government would help build new dwellings and matching facilities and the farmers thus directly move from the places with harsh natural environment to relatively advanced regions and enjoy the public services there.

There are eight projects in the latest Guangdong Poverty Relief policies, one of which is to consolidate the results of relocation by improving living conditions in resettlement areas and support the building of infrastructure in resettlement regions and the ecological restoration of out-migration areas; to arrange "staying with relatives and friends" migration for those scattered poor households who do not have living and production conditions; and to transform the minority poor people with labor capacity who are not willing to relocate into ecological protection staff such as forest rangers by applying eco-compensation mechanism.

Educational Poverty Alleviation: Enhancing Education Level before Implementing Poverty Alleviation

"The Sahara Desert" in Leizhou

Leizhou Peninsula, located in the southernmost point of China, borders on the Beibu Gulf in the west, the South China Sea in the east and is separated by the 18-sea-mile Qiongzhou Strait with Hainan Island to the south. About 5,000 to 6,000 years ago, there were ready human beings on this red earth and it was brought into Huaxia (ancient China) in the Qin dynasty and was the location of the ancient Hepu county governance. Leizhou Peninsula was also an important base for foreign trade in Han dynasty and the original port of "Maritime Silk Road". It was after the Tang dynasty that the governors had the plan of "moving Cantonese to Hezhou" (Hezhou was later changed into Leizhou in the Tang Zhenguan Eighth Year). The southward migration increased year by year after the Song dynasty, which stepped up the development speed of Leizhou Peninsula. The Peninsula people have created various unique intangible cultures in the past hundreds of thousands of years. Leizhou song, performed in the Peninsula's distinct dialect Leiyu, is the country's intangible cultural heritage. And there are great differences between the dialect of Leizhou and those in other parts of Guangdong, especially the relatively richer Pearl River Delta area.

Located in Leizhou Peninsula, Dongtang village has a strange phenomenon: ever since the reform and opening up, no matter how many young labor leave the place to work elsewhere, they would all return to the province-known poor village in the end because they find themselves unsecure to work in places outside their hometown.

According to a survey made in 2010, there were 908 households, 3,957 people in Dongtang, and 2,021 people among 468 households were living under the poverty line, making a poverty rate of over 51%. And as it was said by the World Bank that China's overall poverty rate was around 53%, we could tell the living standards in Dongtang still stood at the level of the 1980s.

Wang Nan has been working as the village secretary for 13 years on this barren land. It was not until 2010 that he made a farewell to cottage room and moved into red brick house with the help of his two brothers.

Why was poverty alive all the time in this small village? And how did poverty alleviation take effect there?

It is necessary to first illustrate the environment in Leizhou by comparing it with the Sahara Desert. The Sahara Desert is located in the north of Africa, stretching from the Mediterranean in the north to the Sudan Prairie in the south. The desert was formed about 250,000,000 years ago and is the second largest desert and the largest gravel desert in the world. Located in the northern Africa, it is regarded as one of the most unsuitable places for biological existence. Leizhou Peninsula is often called by people as the "Sahara Desert" in Leizhou.

The natural environment in Dongtang can be described as "harsh" . The lands are barren and suffer from severe desertification. In rainy seasons, the sea wind brings plentiful rainfall and leaves water stored in the fields, which cannot be emptied for half a year but in some dry months, villagers have to watch the seedlings die.

Since the 21st century, China has invested much capital in agriculture and the purchasing prices for grains have gone up gradually, with the minimum rice price reaching 1 yuan/jin in Guangdong. However, such progress seems to make no benefits to Dongtang villagers, and even in good years they can only feed themselves with the food planted. In fact, villagers are relying on the Heaven rather than fields for food because even in the best years, they can only harvest up to 500 units of food. But in other regions, villagers can harvest more than thousands of units of food with the application of mechanized planting. However, as most people in Dongtang only attend primary or secondary schools, many of them "haven't heard about" scientific farming. In Dongtang, mechanized planting is an untrodden area and in the eyes of the under-educated villagers, new equipment such as tractors and fertilizers are troublesome things.

Before the year 2010, Li Xuegui was utterly destitute and there was no calendar, no clocks in his house. Being an illiterate, Li has been living a life of doing farming work with neighbors in the morning and coming back home at night for many years. In order to increase production with the limited lands, Li had to plant sweet potatoes once she had reaped the rice. Some technicians had told the villagers how to raise yields by scientific farming, but she and her neighbors could not remember and perform it.

At weekends, Li's children had to go back home and do farm work on the fields, and they needed to live in their neighbor's house since there was no vacant beds for them. The family devoted all their efforts to planting and preserving their land because they fed themselves with it and in good years, they might have a good harvest. Unfortunately, almost no families could have left food for sale. Some villagers have tried to plant peanuts or peppers but they just "had passion rather than techniques" and lost money in spite of a year's hard work.

An Outer World
that Cannot Be Fitted into

In the 1990s, millions of workers swarmed into the Pearl River Delta, a paradise filled with job opportunities.

Dongtang villagers were among the migrant workers. The swirling wheels took those with dreams of making money and supporting families to the outer world. However, luck seemed to escape them—no one was heard of making money outside and the migrant workers soon went back to the village.

Over a decade has passed, villagers said nothing had changed but the dirt road leading to the village had been covered with cement.

In the house of Zhengxin, the red bricks bought four years ago were still piled at the corner and already covered with moss. In 2006, the cottage Zheng lived in for several decades were worn down. When it rained outside, there would be a flood in the room. After a heavy rain this year, the cottage underwent a disaster and almost half of it collapsed.

It was in exactly the same year that Zheng Xin's 22-year-old son went to work in Guangdong under the recommendation of friends after graduating from junior high school. The family decided to build a new house considering there would be financial support since their eldest son went to big cities to work. They quickly spent all the 20,000 yuan lent from relatives while their son could hardly feed himself in Guangzhou. The young people, with no understanding of mandarin or specific skills, had to live on picking up rubbish with fellow villagers. The family's dream of building a house was gone and so did their old cottage. Under desperation, they moved to the nearby forest and set up two "wooden tents" with branches. The smaller one was for Zhao Xin's mother and his wife and he lived in the bigger one. Having been working for four years, Zheng Xin's eldest son could only earn a monthly wage of 800 yuan. In his calls with his grandmother, the boy told her he wanted to go back home and do farm work because the outer world was too harsh.

The middle-aged in the village once had the similar experience as Zheng's eldest son. They went to work in the Pearl River Delta or neighboring provinces and came back after at most three years. The fundamental cause for this phenomenon is that Dongtang villagers speak "Leizhou Mandarin" and the heavy accent is hard to be understood. As a result, their promotion is hindered by ineffective communication.

The mouthful of "Leizhou mandarin" originates from Dongtang primary school. On the classes before 2010, the teacher was teaching children Pinyin in mandarin by stressing every single syllable. But as he turned around and shouted "Be quite!" to the students, the accent changed into Leizhou dialect. At that time, both the 301 student and all the teachers were local residents and with less than 1/20 households owning a television and almost none knowing about the Internet, they were helplessly shunned from the outer world.

Most of the teachers in Leizhou stay at the school to teach once they graduated from the sixth grade and get diplomas for refresher courses after years of teaching, so they have missed the prime time to learn mandarin. As a result, "Leizhou mandarin" is handed down from generation to generation. On the surface, however, the rate for primary school students entering secondary school is 100%. As most rural children go to school at an older age and it is "quite common for them to enter primary school at eight", most of the junior school starters in Dongtang are over 16 years old.

The old junior graduates with strong Leizhou accent repeat the path of their father's generation. The difficulties in reality cannot lessen their eagerness for entering the outer world. Throng of Dongtang villagers come back to their hometown with tears in their eyes after a year or two of tough lives in the big cities. They take over the hoes from their father's hands, marry and raise children, and end their lives in poverty and mediocrity.

Made in China 2025 Initiative and Educational Poverty Alleviation

The conception of "Made in China 2025" was first put forward in December, 2014. Four months later, on 5 March, 2015, Premier Li Keqiang came up with the grand strategy when he was making a report on government work on NPC and CPPCC. The strategy is the program of action for the first decade of Chinese government's strategy of building a powerful manufacturing country. The first step is to shift China from a big manufacturing country to a strong one by 2025. The second one is to make China able to compete with developed manufacturing powers by 2035. The third one is to transform China into a leading manufacturing power by 2049.

Qualified professionals are indispensable to complete such an upgrading task of manufacturing industry as "Made in China 2025". As urbanization advances, the large number of migrant workers in Guangdong has the potential of becoming qualified industrial workers. High quality workers are in great demand in the Pearl River Delta. However, poverty prevents those from mountainous areas from learning technical knowledge and getting systematic training. The status quo of education in Dongtang village also reveals the problems facing Guangdong's poverty alleviation work: insufficient input for educational infrastructure, unbalanced allocation of faculty and uncertain prospects for graduates.

For those poor households and their children, it is not a long-run plan to relieve their poverty by simply giving them clothes, food and shelters. To relieve the poor we first need to enhance the educational levels. Actually, all the residents in the mountains know that they need to leave their hometown so as to become rich and that they have to equip themselves with knowledge before leaving. To guarantee the effect of poverty alleviation on "individual" , good mandarin skills and enhanced cultural qualities are the prerequisites.

In December 2009, Shenzhen Pingshan New Area became assistance partners with the four villages in Dongli Town, including Dongtang village. It was acknowledged that professional skills could not be improved if people have low mandarin levels. For the 198 people with work capability in the poor households of Dongtang, Pingshan New Area arranged free technical skill training tours under the principle of "one trained, one employed, one alleviated from poverty" . The area also organized purposefully villagers to work there and master techniques and accumulate experience to make preparation for future returning to the village and achieving integral poverty alleviation.

At the same time, the Dongtang Primary School, standing at the side of the village road, had taken on a new appearance. A reinforced concrete public toilet was built in the southwest of the school with a 33,600 yuan fund from Pingshan New Area. A garbage pool, constructed over the same period, thoroughly settled the 300 teachers' and students' difficulty in using toilet and remarkably improved the school's environment.

Outside the village, some strangers encounter several kids riding bikes and playing around. They think those children can not understand mandarin, just like the adults they meet along the road. To their surprise, one boy suddenly comes near and asks in mandarin: "Where are you going?"

Eliminating Ignorance before Combating Poverty

On 16 October, 2015, Yang Guoqiang, founder of Country Garden Co., Ltd in Shunde, was awarded "China's Poverty Elimination Prize" (Innovation Prize) on the Alleviation and Development High-level Forum. He launched the mutual assistance model of "government and society" in education area. Yang Guoqiang and his daughter have donated over 1.3 billion yuan to Guangdong's poverty alleviation project since 2010. The 800 million donated before had been used for six projects: the green industry poverty relief in Qingyuan, Zhaoqing and Guangzhou, the poverty alleviation in Huaiji county, the poverty alleviation in Timian town, technique and skill trainings in villages, establishment of Guangdong Country Garden Professional School and targeted poverty alleviation.

Born in a poor farmer family in Shunde, Guangdong, Yang hardly wore shoes before he was seventeen. He could never forget that the government exempted his tuition fees of 7 yuan per semester and gave him 2 yuan as grant to let him finish the high school course otherwise he had to drop out of school due to poverty. He deeply felt the positive influence of education upon thoroughly eliminating poverty. Thus, he stepped onto the road of educational poverty elimination after becoming a successful entrepreneur.

After all these years, when Yang Guoqiang recollected his past years of striving, he believed he was driven by the desire for knowledge. To further explain this point, Yang gave us an example: when he and his cousin, now the Chief Financial Officer of Country Garden, received the 2 yuan allowance and exemption of tuition fees, they went to buy a lot of books with the money they had.

In 1997, Yang donated one million yuan and anonymously set up the "Zhongming Scholarship" to support poverty-stricken college students and 8,000 students have benefited from the scholarship in the past 18 years. Yang also established the Guohua Memorial Secondary School with an input of 260 million yuan in 2002, which enrolled extraordinary students from poor families and offered them grant till they got bachelor's, master's or even doctor's degrees. Eleven years later, Yang invested 350 million yuan in starting the Guangdong Country Garden Professional School, where students would be exempted from all expenses and be given subsidies. The school is currently a typical educational poverty alleviation project in Guangdong. Now it has an enrollment of 672 poor students. And after two years of student recruitment, most of the students are Cantonese.

In 2012, Yang Guoqing developed another way of educational poverty alleviation in Shuitou Town, Fogang County, Qingyuan. He started a "technique and skill training project in villages" by moving the professional classrooms to villages. The project targeted the working-age population between 16 and 60 years old, offering them free skill training and helping the trainees to get jobs by contacting personnel companies and employing units. For the last three years, the project have trained 16,469 people, with

8,150 obtaining 9 kinds of job qualification certificates for forklift drivers, electricians, nurses and so on and 3,828 working in the cities under recommendation.

Yang believes, on the one hand, that the college need to systematically cultivate labourers with high quality and proficient skills and on the other hand, that people's biased attitudes towards vocational schools should be changed as more high-level employment taking place among those who attend such schools.

Yang's ideas were verified to be true according to a survey made by the Ministry of Human Resources and Social Security. It was said that among the 225,000,000 second-industry working population, only 119,000,000 were skilled craftsmen. Up to over 400 million working force was needed for senior mechanic in manufacturing industry alone and the severe conflict between the demand and supply of skilled craftsmen hindered the advancement of corporation technological upgrade. Yang Guoqiang, as a member of the national committee of CPPCC, handed in "A Proposal for Encouraging and Instructing Private Enterprises to Actively Join in Educational Poverty Alleviation" on the 2015 CPPCC.

Emphasizing professional educational poverty alleviation has gained support from institutions on the national level. The State Council has issued a regulation which set up clear goals for establishing the modern professional education system.

Although educational alleviation requires heavy input, troublesome process and long period of time and is hard to persevere, it has a notable effect in realizing "cultivate one person, relieve one household from poverty" policy and thoroughly preventing poverty from being handed down to next generations. Undoubtedly, it can actualize a win-win relationship among individuals, families and society. In Yang's 18 years of educational poverty alleviation, around 40,000 people have got rid of poverty. Yang said: "The wealth I gained is the thing I hold in custody for society, so it's natural to help others when I'm capable. I'm just performing my responsibility. I always feel the most important thing in a man is his qualities and educational poverty alleviation is 'teaching a man how to fish'."

▲ Implement the principle of eliminating ignorance before combating poverty. Volunteers of poverty elimination are building mobile library for children in mountainous areas with donated books.

Medical Poverty Alleviation: Eliminating the Root of Poverty for 600,000 People

Illness Hinders the Steps towards Wealth

Health and sanitation holds a crucial position in relieving or even eliminating poverty. Margaret Chan Fung Fu-chun, secretary-general of the World Health Organization, pointed out in her speech on the 2015 Poverty Alleviation and Development Forum that sanitation, health and poverty were closely interrelated. Poverty will influence people's health and things such as poor, unhealthy, unsanitary environment, lack of nutrition and misuse of medication and tobaccos will challenge one's spiritual and physical health. It is evident that people with better body can get rid of poverty more easily.

In the 1.765 million relatively poor population in Guangdong, the proportion of people who suffer from poverty due to illness is up to 36.2%. It means that illness has become the biggest stumbling block on the way of Guangdong's effort in getting rid of poverty for those in mountainous areas. One person falls sick, the family falls apart. So how to offer sufficient medical treatment to farmers is a major obstacle for Guangdong's poverty relief work.

In southern Guangdong, villagers from Xikou, Meizhou could hardly feed the whole family with the four pieces of land per person. As there is a severe unbalance between demand and supply, the only solution is to "find work outside the mountains". Xikou villagers have long known this is the way out of poverty, but not all of them can leave their hometown and work in the counties or travel further to the Pearl River Delta. In some households, the family members suffer from diseases and lose labor capability. As a result, they don't have affluent workforce for the outer world and the families are thus dragged back from their way of accumulating wealth by the cirrus-like illness.

Diseases sweep over these families, leaving only one or two solitary members who are capable to work. Xikou village is located in the south of Qingxi town, Dapu county, Meizhou. Prior to the year 2010, the village had a population of 1,748 and a total of 181 poor households and 726 poor people earned an annual income of less than 1,500 yuan. There were 242 units of paddy fields, and most people had to work as migrant workers since each one could be allocated with only 4 pieces of land.

Having worked outside for 30 years, Liu Changxi returned to Xikou with almost nothing, and the adobe house aside of the 332 Provincial Road was all he had. He has been striving to change his destiny for half of his life, only to find himself defeated by illness.

Liu Changxi was among the group of the earliest migrant workers in the local area after the reform and opening up. In 1997, Liu left his home, but the elementary school graduate could only travel around and work with low wages because he failed to enter the state-owned mining factory. Under someone's recommendation, Liu was hired by a local in Longmen county to take care of the commercial crop on the mountains. Ten years later, Liu married a woman 15 years younger than him in his fifties, who was a widow with epilepsy.

Marriage, while bringing Liu a sense of belonging, doomed his improving life. His wife suffered a lot from the illness and Liu travelled everywhere to find medical treatment for her. "New rural cooperative medical system" hasn't been popularized at the beginning of the 1990s, and Liu was suffocated by the dual burden of medical fees and travelling expenses.

In 2010, the 76-year-old Liu died in his combat with poverty and illness and his path was followed by the 41-year-old Ding Ruihui. After his wife's death in 2006, Ding abandoned his identity as a rural migrant worker and took up farm work in order to take care of his elderly parents and three young daughters. Before his wife passed away, their life was just better off and they built two brick houses in the village, but Ding owed a 40,000 yuan debt to pay for his wife's treatment and he couldn't pay it off after four years of his wife's death.

Ding had a family of six people and owned only three pieces of land. He had to work part time in Chayang and Qingxi town after busy seasons. Financing his parents' medical treatment and his daughter's living expenses in secondary school with an unstable income, Ding scarcely had extra money at hand.

Xikou is just an epitome of the poverty-stricken people caused who suffer from illness. Some migrant workers do succeed in getting rid of poverty, but others could hardly earn a good salary because they are under-educated. Li Qingxiang, cadre of poverty-relief work, believes that since currently most young workers from the poor mountainous areas only graduate from secondary school and complete the basic compulsory education, they could only do the bottom layer jobs when they're in the outside world.

Illness-related poverty has mainly two causes. On the one hand, farmers could not afford the medical expenses due to vulnerable economic base. On the other hand, illness deprives the family members of their labor capability and leads to family's living standards falling under poverty line when there is only one grown-man supporting the whole family.

Li Qingxiang said: "Some family members lose their labor capability or even die when they catch certain diseases, which in the end leads to the family's worsening situation, and such households account for the majority of poor families. And a major difficulty for the anti-poverty project is the poverty-returning phenomenon due to illness.

In the end all the reasons for poverty make up one clue: farmers migrant work in other places because they can't make a fortune through traditional farming due to insufficient lands-migrant workers have a low wage and live in poverty for lack of cultural knowledge-and some families have to bear the burden of expenses for medical treatment or lose working labor (infected with disease or die), and thus become the poorest groups of people.

The Ups and Downs in Rural Medical Care

Seven years ago, for the 300 people production team Liu Changxi worked in, only one clinic was equipped to take care of them. Back then, the status quo of the medical conditions in poverty-stricken mountainous areas was that most primary physicians were from junior colleges or technical secondary schools, so it would be impossible for them to cure all kinds of illness.

Tu Qizhi, dean of a health-center, felt quite helpless when speaking of the embarrassing situations in the past seven or eight years as they didn't have enough health resources. At that time, he only had a staff team of 10 doctors and three nurses.

Besides a shortage of manpower, the health center was also poorly-equipped, with a black and white ultrasound machine being the most advanced facility. And when the elderly doctors retired, successors could not be found. Tu used to ask for personnel from Dapu Sanitary Bureau, but he knew the possibility of ever finding one was rare. He explained it was because the low salary offered by them was of little attraction.

Dean Tu then had a monthly wage of about 1,500 yuan, and the doctors graduated from junior colleges and technical secondary schools earned 700 yuan and 600 yuan respectively.

With a widening gap between the wages of county health centers and urban hospitals, many experienced doctors flock to cities and fewer people go to clinics to treat their illness.

As an elementary healthcare worker, Tu empathizes farmers' difficulty in seeing a doctor.

Currently, China's basic healthcare insurance is mainly divided into three categories: working people healthcare insurance, medical insurance for urban residents and new rural cooperative medical system (NCMS). Among these, medical insurance for urban residents are paid by government finance and residents themselves and managed by the Bureau of Human Resources and Social Security while the NCMS is paid by government and farmers and managed by the Bureau of Health and Family Planning.

In the 1970s, China's rural cooperative medical service system, county-countryside-village medical care system in rural areas and barefoot doctors were considered as the "three magic weapons" for solving the lack of doctors and medication in villages and protecting public's health. The rural cooperative model was highly commended by the World Health Organization and the World Bank as "the model of largest health benefits with least input" and was introduced to the developing countries. Cooperative medical service was written into the Constitution of PRC in 1978 and prior to the reform of rural production responsibility regulations in agriculture, the coverage of rural medical service had been up to 80% to 90%.

After the 1980s, villages initiated the household contract responsibility system. People's commune was abolished, production team disassembled, leading to a quick shrink of rural collective economy. This was soon followed by the disintegration of cooperative medical service system. As most village clinics and cooperative medical service stations became the private clinic of country doctors, the phenomenon of farmers' lack of doctors and medication reappeared. According to a survey, the cooperative medical service coverage dropped dramatically from 68.8% in 1980 to below 20% in 1983. It was said by the 1985's statistics that the villages implementing cooperative medical service went straight down from 90% to 5%. The Chinese government have again attempted to reconstruct the rural cooperative system by carrying out "privately run under state ownership and voluntary participation" in the 1990s, but they failed to reach the expected desire for recovery and construction as the system designed didn't clearly state the government's entity responsibility in securing the society. One set of data can be used to illustrate the embarrassing situation of rural cooperative medical service: while in 1979 the national finance health care costs granted 100 million yuan to the cooperative system, the figure dropped to 35 million in 1992, which only accounted for 0.36% of the total health care costs.

At the beginning of this century, with an increasingly unbalanced development in urban and rural areas, China restarted the construction of rural cooperative medical service system in October 2002 and renamed it as a new system. The new rural cooperative system adopted a financing mechanism of individual payment, collective support and government funding. The cooperative medical service funding was mainly used to subsidize farmers' large-sum or hospitalized medical bills, forbidding overspending or excessive balance. The updated NCMS, besides targeting at outpatient and hospitalization services, also includes the insurance for serious illness. Take Guangzhou as an example, nowadays rural residents only have to pay 100 yuan/year for the system, then they can get a grant of 340 yuan/year from local governments, a reimbursement limit of 50% and 70% for outpatient and hospitalization services. If they catch some serious illness, they can enjoy an over 50% reimbursement for the self-paid expenses. The maximum limit is 150,000 yuan/year.

At the beginning of 2016, Guangdong province actualized the integration of rural and urban medical care insurance systems. After this, the scales and medication catalogues of local fixed medical care institutions have witnessed an evident enlargement. Now urban and rural residents use the same basic medicine insurance catalogue, and the reimbursable medication categories for farmers have increased.

Medical Poverty Alleviation: A "One Package Service" to Relieve Poverty

Besides the enhancement of new rural cooperative medical system, Guangdong is also using new systems and technologies to solve the problems in medical poverty alleviation.

Liannan is a poverty-stricken region in Guangdong province and there are considerable gaps between Liannan's and the average provincial medical and health standards. Three big hospitals were once located here, but due to the limitations in medical technologies and environment, an estimated rate of 40% of locals would go to the neighboring Lizhou or Lianshan to see doctors. How to have the patients go to local hospitals to see doctors?

Officials in Guangdong College of Pharmacy suggest that the college's assistance to Liannan People's Hospital is out of the accountability of public welfare and social responsibility rather than commercial purposes. After the collocation, the hospital adopted a management mode of de-administrative corporate representative, and set up a decision-making level board and a supervisory committee supervising the former's exercise of power. All the positions in the hospital were de-administrated and rankings were removed, with leading groups appointed by the board. The management team and technical experts sent by the Guangdong College of Pharmacy also greatly enhanced the standards of Liannan Hospital.

Besides the new rural cooperative medical system and effective medical resources allocation, new technologies also put forward solutions to the problems of medical poverty alleviation. The 91-year-old Liang Bao had a stroke six years ago and was half-paralyzed, he could only move around in his just over 10 square meters room and was unable to take a sunbath in front of his house, not to mention going to see a doctor. On 16 October, 2016, a Yangshan family doctor team launched by Yanshan Medical Group of Guangdong No.2 People's Hospital and Guangdong Network Hospital arrived at the Fan village (Yangshan county, Qingyuan) Liao Bao lived and signed a contract with him to provide him with free targeted treatment. It was a new welfare offered by provincial No.2 People's Hospital of Yangshan Hospital Group.

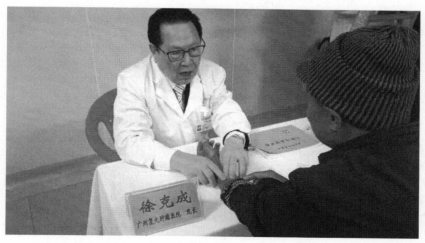

▲ Xu Kecheng, a renowned doctor, is carrying out a free clinic to relieve regional poverty. Free clinic in medical poverty alleviation campaigns let the renowned doctors go to grassroot levels to provide high quality medical services for local residents.

The data released by Guangdong Poverty Alleviation Office in August 2016 showed that the major three reasons causing poverty among the relatively poor households in the province were illness (36.2%), lack of labor (23.3%) and disability (19.9%). Yangshan is just an epitome of poor mountainous regions. There are 159 villages in Yanghshan, and Zhou Qiru, the Dean of Guangdong Network Hospital, and his staff screened out over 2,000 illness-related poor households by traveling from villages to villages.

In order to have good quality medical resources come to the grassroots and improve country's medical and health care services levels, Yangshan Medical Group of Guangdong No.2 People's Hospital proposed to use "internet and public health care" to carry out medical poverty alleviation.

Experts find that, in Yangshan, there are many residents like Liang Bao, who cannot travel far to see doctors and must be provided with door-to-door service. The online and offline healthcare management team from the Guangdong Network Hospital have started a "one package" service for these people. The family doctor team is composed of village doctors, doctors from township health centers and the Guangdong Network Hospital and party members and experts from Yangshan Medical Group of Guangdong No.2 People's Hospital. After signing an agreement, doctors will complete the establishment of health profiles for these households and track and update the profiles on time. Besides, they will also provide some individualistic preferential services such as tracking the diseases of the elderly, the young and women, serious and chronic diseases and sharing provincial, prefectural, town and village-level medical resources. The over

2,000 "illness-caused poverty" households in Yangshan will all sign agreements with the family doctor team. Within two years, the sicken members in these families will get free and concise treatment and get health management, which aims at improving their living standards fundamentally and let them get rid of poverty.

Let us turn back to the story of Liu Changxi. Now he has joined the new rural cooperative medical system and with the coverage of serious illness insurance, the reimbursement proportion for his wife's disease has drastically increased and the plight of his family has relieved a lot. In the meantime, as the medical power comes down to villages, two community doctors who have received professional training have arrived at the production brigade Liu Changxi's in. As a result, he needn't go to the town dozens of miles away to see doctors.

Establishing Transportation System to Relieve Poverty: Building a Good Road for Villages—A Way Out and A Way to Survive

Smooth Artery
but Blocked Blood Capillary

Ever since China's reform and opening up, farmers have learned many lessons on their way to wealth, and the most notable one is "If you want to be rich, build a road first. And road is the criteria of whether a region is rich or not". From this, we can tell the great importance of village roads in China's economic development. Transportation is crucial for economic growth and keeping village roads open is a key for rural economic development.

Guangdong, as the one of the earliest provinces launching reform and opening up, has been playing a leading role in the construction of infrastructure such as transportation. By the end of 2015, the traffic mileage of Guangdong highway has reached 7,018 miles, being the first province in China that outnumbers 7,000 miles. Guangdong has realized the goal of "making every county connected to highways", and has 17 routes leading out of the province and over three land routes connecting to the neighboring provinces. While the eastern, western and northern parts of Guangdong have an evidently improved highway network and a transport mileage of 3,282 miles, an extensive and balanced highway backbone network is basically taking into shape. The figures show the great investment and achievement of Guangdong's road construction. However, such constructions mostly take place in highly-developed areas such as the

Pearl River Delta, and for the mountainous areas in the eastern, western and northern parts of Guangdong, there is still a lot that needs to be done for transportation infrastructure construction.

Located in Heyuan, Yangmei village used to be a place that was filled with over-aged youth who couldn't find wives due to the blocking traffic. "Even though the boys have good looks, that's useless for helping them get married." When asked about the cause of poverty, all the villagers pointed out it was because of "the worn-out roads".

The difficulty in getting out of the village was the residents' deepest memories. In earlier years, it took Yangmei villagers a long time to arrive at Heyuan. Leaving at 7.30 in the morning, villagers had to travel on the mountain road for two hours, walked out of the eastern mountain to arrive at Xichang Harbor, took a ferry-boat and reached Heyuan at 12.30 at noon. If they failed to settle their affairs in the afternoon, they had to stay at a hotel and leave the other day.

Villagers Are Longing for Good Roads

Zhan Shiyuan once planted dozens of units of fruit trees in 2001, but he told us: "Due to the worn-out mountain road, the buyers don't want to come to the village and when they do come, they would demand a lower price. For example, one could spend a few dimes to buy the goods that are sold at 1 yuan outside." Almost all villagers lose money for their investment because of the inconvenient transportation. No matter for vegetables or fruit, the delivery truck would be waiting outside the mountains, and villagers have to carry the goods on a seven miles journey eastward. Yangmei village has a broken gun carrier retired from the troop and it is the only vehicle to deliver goods through the mud roads. The villagers have to spend 150-200 yuan for every delivery, and this covers cost of labor, truck-rental fees and expenses for wait times.

In 2008, a farmer from Heshikeng village, Xichang Town successfully cultivated glossy ganoderma in the reservoir area and thus earned a considerable income. Then the plantation of glossy ganoderma was popularized all over the town and Dongyuan county even named Xichang as "glossy ganoderma specialized town" . The cultivation of glossy ganoderma seemed to overnight become the magic weapon for Yangmei villagers to get rid of poverty. In the first year, the planters earn thousands of yuan. Other villagers rushed forward the next year and the dozens of growers had 12 units of plantation altogether. In 2009, villager Li Yamin used six Dongfeng trucks to deliver wood, spent 6,000 yuan on seedlings and cultivated over 2,500 jins of glossy ganoderma.

However, Yangmei villagers were painful to learn that the seedlings in the wooden stakes were dead by May and piles of wood, steamed and inserted with seedlings, could only be used to make fire. The villagers said: "We still haven't figured out the causes by now. Some say the woods were infected, but no experts would come here and give us instructions."

Through their efforts, the 10.5-mile country road leading to the town to the east side of the village was finally open to traffic in 2007. But for the 7-mile economic way in the west, the villagers failed to get project approvals after several attempts. The researchers of the National Leading Group of Poverty Alleviation and Development discovered from the survey of eastern provinces' poverty relief work that the infrastructure construction in Guangdong poor areas was highly backward, which failed to fit with industrial development and there was still a lot of heavy work unfinished for improving poverty-stricken people's living standards.

It was not until 2012 that Yangmei village got approved for the construction of the economic road in the west side with the help of poverty alleviation institutions. The village had the road open to traffic by the end of that year with the 240 million funding.

A Good Road Is A Way Out and A Way to Survive

Sishui is an assisted village in the last round's (2013-2015) poverty alleviation campaign household-and individual-targeted and has got rid of poverty by now. Wang Manxiu, provincial NPC member, party branch secretary and director of village committee of Sishui, concluded from the experience of poverty alleviation work that country roads had to be built in order to help poor villagers accumulate wealth. Sishui villagers mainly planted vegetables and trees, but the goods could only rot in the fields because there were no roads for dealers and delivery. Many poor villages face the same circumstances as Sishui: they are not scarce in resources or industries, but they couldn't sell their good quality agricultural products or develop and promote tourism resources because of inaccessible transportation. The farmers are living a worsening life as natural organic food rot in the lands and beautiful natural sceneries are hidden behind mountains since farmers can't go out and enterprises can't get in.

In order to propel rural economic development, the locals need to increase investment in country road construction, enhance environment for transportation and smooth the way for the adaptation of rural industrial structure and commodity circulation to promote farmers' earnings.

If Guangdong wants to lead in establishing a moderately prosperous society in 2018, poverty alleviation is a key battle for it to win.

▲ The photo is a scene of the mutual-assistance poverty alleviation and development project bewteen Dongyong Town, Fanyu District and Paitan Town. On 21 June, 2016, in Chinese Yam Horizontal Planting Technology Agricultural Demonstration Base, a farmer is pruning branches for a well-grown Chinese yam. Now, Guangzhou is financing eight poor counties to get rid of poverty by building public facilities and establishing new economic industries. (Photo taken by Shao Quanda)

"Implementing Infrastructure Construction Poverty Alleviation Project" is clearly stated as one of the eight Guangdong's poverty alleviation projects. The project aims at not only building roads, but also establishing an effectively interconnected transportation system. Besides offering paths for people to travel through, these roads are also expected to develop industries, vitalize resources, increase incomes for the poor villages.

On the basis of opening highways in every county, Guangdong Provincial Transportation Bureau has drawn up a plan of further enhancing highway network in poor regions and establishing more roads leading to these regions by 2018. The project, focusing on reconstructing county roads, tends to improve the country road construction in poor areas.

The village He Guifang (member of the National People's Congress, party branch secretary and director of village committee of Shanlian village) comes from used to be called as the "Siberia" of Liannan because it had a backward transportation system, blocked information source and laggard development. Over the years, under He's advocation, the roads have been connected, electricity are on, development speeds up and villagers' living standards improve. He believes that the key for Guangdong's improving the production and living standards in poor mountainous areas lies in making up the shortage in rural development. He Youlin, member of the National People's Congress, former principal of Zhongshan Memorial Secondary School, said that: "It's essential to build good roads for villages. For villagers, a good road is not only a way out, but also a way to survive."

Financial Poverty Alleviation: Stepping up the Way of Overcoming Poverty

Lack of Funding in Agriculture: A Financial Deficit in Spring Ploughing

Speaking of the poverty-stricken areas in Guangdong, the first that comes to people's minds is those in the eastern, western and northern parts of Guangdong. However, poverty also exists in the Pearl River Delta. Jinkeng village is one example. Located in Dongcheng Town in Jiangmen Wuyi areas, the village has an area of 104,000 square kilometers and in its five natural villages, there are 471 households and a total population of 1,499. The villagers make their living mainly on planting rice with low added value. Villagers and the village committee have an average annual income of 3,100. Besides starting business abroad, some villagers also work in Enping, Jiangmen, Zhongshan and Guangzhou.

Lack of funding is one of the major issues restricting the agricultural development in Jinkeng.

In 1995, a banking crisis outbroke in Enping as a result of attracting deposits by high interests. The banks went bankrupt one by one and there was a recession in the development of local financial institutions for more than a decade. The local commercial banks cut down dramatically its service network stations, coming down from 266 before the financial crisis to 43 now.

In rural areas, as Enping's urban and rural cooperatives have been canceled, financial services could only depend on postal savings banks since other financial institutions either don't have agricultural financial services or "only permit deposits but don't offer loans" . According to statistics, the local loan balance was only 480,000 yuan by the end of 2007, accounting for barely 0.03% of the agricultural loans in Jiangmen areas.

Jinkeng is just an epitome of the poor villages in Guangdong. Since 1998, the support for issues of agriculture, farmer and rural area has almost been blank. There was even lack of financial support for the basic rice planting. It was estimated by Enping Agricultural Bureau that in 2006, the budget for spring ploughing would be about 50.4 million yuan, but farmers had only 11.8 million at hand, so there would still be a financing deficit up to 38.6 million.

Incomprehensive Agricultural Insurance: Farmers Taking on All Financial Risks

"Enping is located in the Pearl River Delta, so there is a broad market for planting and farming industries with the convenient transportation," said by Feng Langqi, deputy director general of Enping Agricultural Bureau. He believed that planting and farming required not only technologies and fundings but also agricultural insurance.

But agricultural insurance is incomplete and incomprehensive. It is known that since 2006, Enping insurance industry has seldom invested in the agricultural projects with low benefits and now, due to long time loss, it has stopped some tentative agriculture insurance. The lack of agriculture insurance to effectively withstand risks and unestablished correspondent risk compensation system further restrict financial institution's investment in agricultural construction and this has fallen into a vicious circle.

In 2006, Professor Yunus, known as "the poor's banker", won Nobel Peace Prize for his establishment of rural banks. The news inspired Chinese people and a new reform policy for opening rural financial market was brewing.

In December 2016, China Banking Regulatory Commission introduced a new policy which for the first time allowed industrial and private capitals to establish banks in rural areas and advocated setting up three financial institutions: village banks, finance corporations and rural mutual cooperatives. This attempt was considered as the ice-breaking move in the fourth-round of China's rural finance reformation.

Zhang Yuanhong, researcher of the Rural Development Institute of Chinese Social Academy College, said that: "Petty loan is very difficult to apply and this is a ubiquitous phenomenon in China rural areas." He also suggested with profits being the main targets of banks and a more intensive cost settlement, dispersed rural outlets were contracted and the examination and approval authority was centralized. Now, banking outlets under county-levels basically don't have the power to examine and approve loans.

Let Finance
Return to Rural Areas

In fact, the lack of financial service in villages has already drawn attention from in society.

In 2009, there were over 60 villages with non-banking financial institution networks, located mainly in eastern, western and northern Guangdong and regions with underdeveloped economy or small-scale financial industries. Between 2010 and 2013, Guangdong had gradually filled the gap of non-banking financial institution networks in these villages by impelling new pilot types and scopes of rural finance institutions and encouraging commercial banks and rural credit cooperatives to set up new outlets.

The model of village banks were also introduced to China and piloted within a small range. By the end of 2007, Guangdong had officially started to make plans for the pilot work of new rural financial institutions and Enping and Ruyuan were selected as the first pilot regions. In March 2009, HSBC Enping Village Bank had a grand opening and it introduced a "corporation plus farmers" petty loan service. It provided loans for farmers and distributors who had frequent business transactions with the local leading enterprises, focusing on meeting the financial demands of Enping's rural and urban residents and rural micro and middle and small-sized enterprises.

In order to bring development to agriculture, farmer and rural area, China is currently proposing a series of policies: encouraging commercial bank share system to extend to countryside, initiatively providing farmers with petty loans and helping develop production. In the well-prepared and highly-developed regions, banking outlets are set up to facilitate farmers with loan transactions. Implementing new rural financial system and establishing rural household organizations and petty loan corporations are measures to facilitate farmers' loan-applying.

Some poor regions lack in effective mode of economic development, thus financial capitals are hard to be invested and sustainability is not

▲ On 14 June, 2012, municipal leaders of Peijiang District, Jiangmen are spearheading an effort to donate for Poverty Alleviation Campaign. Members from all social sectors in Jiangmen actively participate in the campaign. On the day before, a written proposal was released to encourage people to join in the activity. Photo taken by Chen Zhuoda.

formed. Facing the chronic problems that hinder poor areas from overcoming poverty, such as difficulties in mortgage guarantee, insufficient guarantee pawn and unqualified borrowers, Guangdong banking industry has innovatively launched financial products suitable for rural comprehensive reformation and given a helped ease farmers' difficulties in borrowing money from banks.

In order to clear up the difficulties in guarantee, Guangdong Qingyuan Bank has launched a new "flow loan" targeting at 800 households with contractual rights of land. Li Liang, vice president of the Qingyuan Outlet of Agricultural Bank of China, suggested that: "On the basis of issuing certificates for contractual rights of land, farmers can apply for loans from village banks as needed and transform land resources to loan capitals."

After learning about local conditions, Guandong Yingde Rural Credit Cooperative released a loan product "adapted for farmers" , which moderately relaxed the restriction that borrowers must register in industry and commerce department. A credit line of two million yuan was allocated to farmlands from the rural credit cooperative in Yewu village, Shigutang Town, Yingde, to support land circulation and enhance land utilization rate.

To realize targeted poverty alleviation, Guangdong Provincial Party Committee starts a mode of "staying in village for poverty relief plus establishing cards for archives" and actively promotes "planning for every household and responsibility on every individual" in the province. A fixed three-year period is set for residential poverty alleviation groups to help villagers get rid of poverty.

This mode provides specialized petty loans for archived poor households to ensure funds are used for production and employment. Guangdong Banking Regulatory Commission encourages banking financial institutions to provide loans of no more than 50,000 yuan and within three years for archived poor households who have the willingness to borrow, the potential to start a business and professional skills on the basis of accurately evaluating these households' credit ratings and repayment abilities. The loans can be used to satisfy their demands for production, start-ups, employment and relocation and are with preferential interest rates.

Technology
Accelerates Poverty
Alleviation

Poor Household Selling
Cherry Tomatoes on Taobao

On the Spring Festival of 2006, Super Cold Wave stroke southern China, and most regions in Guangdong was attacked by snow, resulting in the reduced production of weather-dependent farm produce. However, in places such as Zhanjiang, Qingyuan, instead of getting drastically shrinking earnings, some farmers from poor villages even obtained better incomes than ever. It is the "E-commerce Poverty Alleviation" and "Mobile Internet Poverty Alleviation" advocated and spread out by cadres of poverty relief campaign that have brought this change to villagers.

Tangtou villager Luo Ruting has received several boxes of orders for cherry tomatoes just after the Spring Festival and was preparing to harvest fruit in the fields for delivery. Due to the cold weather some seedlings were dry and shrunken. "We didn't have much fruit this year. If we pick some up this morning, then it can be delivered to Guangzhou in the afternoon." Luo casually picked up some bunches of light-red cherry tomatoes and told us: "Fruits sold on market are picked up before they are fully mature because they will naturally become ripe on the way of transportation so that buyer can have the best taste."

The breed of cherry tomato Luo Ruting plants is called "Millennium". It was introduced to Tangtou village from Hainan in 2014 by the poverty relief team in Zhanjiang when they found the information on E-commerce platform. By the introduction of "Millennium" , the embarrassing situation of Tangtou's cherry tomatoes began to change.

By 2013, Luo could barely earn enough money to pay for his wife's medical expenses and children' s tuition fees from the tens of thousands of units of "Wanfu" cherry tomatoes he planted because wholesalers always cut down the purchasing prices. Luo Zhu, committee member of village party branch said: "In the past, cherry fruit could only be sold at fifty cents per jin, but now the purchasing price for Millennium is at least one yuan, one can earn 15,000 yuan for every unit of fruit."

Luo Ruting, who used to be unfamiliar with smart phones, is now proficient in operating E-commerce processes and is responsible for taking orders and organizing delivery. He showed us the page of an online shop called "Zhanjiang Residential Poverty Alleviation Group Franchised Store", which has a wide variety of agricultural produce.

"The signals in the fields aren't so good so we usually check orders on the computer of the village committee," said Luo. He also told us since there is only one computer in the committee, it is planning to buy some new computers with the municipal grants.

He said, with a sense of proud: "Our cherry fruit is the best seller on the market and we have orders from Beijing, Tianjin and Shanghai." Now, the sources of Tangtou's cherry fruit orders have covered the Pearl River Delta. Once receiving an order, Luo will organize purchase and send the products by delivery or shuttle bus. He took scores of orders and went to Guangzhou for four times to deliver goods in December 2015 alone.

Cen Yukang is a cadre of Tangtou's poverty alleviation group and the initiator of "farm produce E-commerce" . In the eyes of the villagers, he is a capable young man with medium height, a pair of glasses and a gentle look. Cen thinks the land conditions in Tangtou are very bad since most of them are unfertile sands and the village has an underdeveloped agricultural irrigation system. To Cen, with 105 poor households out of the 303 households in the village, the load of poverty alleviation task is very heavy.

"After arriving at the village the biggest problem we found was that farmers couldn't learn about the news on the market and they used the old planting technologies to plant agricultural products, including cherry fruit," said Cen. "In the past the seedlings of cherry fruit were all provided by buyers, and besides forcing down prices, they would also deduct a fee of 10% of rotten fruit. Even though some farmers could make a profit, that was not enough for them to get rid of poverty."

Cen was reminded of the vigorous developing trend of mobile Internet in big cities. And on 25 March, 2014, "Tangtou Poverty Alleviation Farm Produce Franchised Store" was officially launched on Taobao and Tangtou thus became the first village that made attempts to relieve poverty by using E-commerce.

According to the notice of China's Ministry of Industry and Information, the domestic users of mobile phone and mobile Internet will reach 1.28 billion and 980 million respectively in 2016. Mobile Internet has exerted a profound influence upon people's lives.

Taobao is a highly popular online retail platform in China owned by

Alibaba Group, a company listed in America. At present, the website has nearly 500 million registered users, over 60 million fixed visitors every day, more than 800 million items in the online shops and averagely sells 48,000 products per minute. And the daily active users on Wechat have reached 670 million. Now people in big and mid-size cities needn't bring cash and credit cards when they go out since consuming places such as restaurants, clothes shops and supermarkets are connected with Internet payment, and consumers can use mobile phones to complete payment even in hospitals, taxis, parking lots and highways.

Cen told us: "At first, the farmers and poor households in the village

▲ E-commerce changes the sales model of farm produce. Farmers use E-commerce to expand market and realize poverty alleviation.

don't know about E-commerce and they think it is too virtual to actually help them do business." In order to let villagers trust "E-commerce" , Cen met up with the biggest local purchaser and cooperated with him by selling cherry tomatoes for poor households on Taobao. It turned out that they helped sell 30,000 jins of "Wanfu" cherry tomatoes in the first half of 2014 alone. At the same time, Cen and the other members learned from the Internet about the "Millennium" cherry tomato in Hainan, which had a higher value as few places in China planted it. So the residential cadres bought grafted seedlings from Hainan, constructed a 100-unit of "Millennium" base and invited experts from Hainan to give technological training to poor households working in the base. After the New Year's Day of 2015, a large amount of "Millennium" cherry fruit was on the market and sold in Taobao shops, attracting plenty of buyers. In the same year, the base earned an income of over 200 million yuan, with 700,000 yuan paying to poverty-stricken farmers as salaries for picking and packaging. In January 2016, the purchasing price for the cherry tomato was up to 7.5 yuan per jin. Since October 2015, almost every villager had begun to plant "Millennium" and the planting area had increased from 100 to 350 units of fields.

As early as October 2014, the farm produce experience of Tangtou village was promoted to all the 95 poverty-stricken villages in Zhanjiang by the residential poverty alleviation team and the name of the Taobao shop was converted into "Zhanjiang Residential Poverty Alleviation Franchised Store" . In the shop, all the farm products from the 95 villages are shown.

Things like cherry fruit, muskmelon, black rice, red rice, black goat, pitaya and seafood can all be found.

Now, all the farmers on Leizhou Peninsula are starting to plant "Milennium" cherry fruit and the planting areas have reached over 3,000 units of fields. Through E-commerce Poverty Alleviation, the cadres and villagers have built bases for green date, muskmelon and pitaya, with the areas of over 6,000 units. Besides, they have also brought in some good quality farm produce such as black rice, red rice and East No.1 honeydew melon and produced well-received sesame and peanut oil.

By the end of February 2016, by connecting with the markets in the Pearl River Delta, Yangzte River Delta and Beijing-Tianjin- Hebei Region, the online and offline sales volume of the agricultural produce in Zhanjiang areas had outnumbered tens of millions yuan. The residential poverty alleviation team in Zhanjiang also established a mode of "E-commerce platform + Storage and processing industrial base + cooperatives + farmers" . This mode had provided a good platform for local poor villages to establish a steady and effective poverty relief system in the long run. It was estimated that 30,000 poverty-stricken households in the Zhanjiang regions had benefited from E-commerce Poverty Alleviation.

Now Tangtou villagers like Luo Ruting and Luo Zhu have been familiar with the processes of selling agricultural products online and the three-year "E-commerce Poverty Alleviation" has brought a huge "E-commerce effect" in the 95 poor villages in Zhanjiang. Residential cadres also help villagers establish a farmers' specialized cooperative comprised of 12 households, which have been leading the development for another 88 households.

From May to August in 2015, Cen Yukang was invited by Shenzhen Training Base of the State Council National Cadres in Poverty-stricken Areas to teach E-commerce poverty alleviation to cadres in seven provinces and districts— Xizang, Yunnan, Jiangxi, Henan, Hunan, Hubei and Guangdong. In the eyes of Cen, E-commerce poverty alleviation was just an exploration to "Internet + Agriculture" mode. Only by the propulsion from the national level could the technological revolution of farm produce in poverty-stricken areas be truly carried out.

He believed the officials should establish an agricultural database as soon as possible, which should be open to agricultural enterprises and common farmers. He said: "For big E-commerce platforms, statistics such as climates, farm produce prices, comparisons among regional products and seedlings sold by sellers should be accessible to farmers. If not, then the government can buy these data from the platforms and make them open to farmers."

"Village Head's Rice" on Suning.com

Located in Chonglou town, Taishan, Qianfeng is a poverty- stricken village where residents make their living on farming. How to better sell the rice villagers plant has been a "long-existing difficult" problem. Due to the flowing back of the sea water and large portion of salt land, the collective income of the village has been stagnant. Three years ago, Jiangmen residential poverty alleviation group arrived here and has been working out different ways to help villagers eliminate the difficulties in selling farm produce.

The team leader of Chongfeng's poverty alleviation group Tan Junyan found that most villagers failed to take the initiative. As a result, the group invited a new village lead Liao Jieliang, a young man of the generation after 80s. Leaving his hometown as a migrant worker at a young age, Liao has always dreamed of applying his experience accumulated in the outer world to construct his village. Liao learned that the 1,800 people in Qianfeng village had a total of 1,700 units of fields and that was an average of less than one unit per person. Besides these, there were also 1300 units of banana patches and 280 units of forest. Apart from the elderly and kids, 60% of the young people were migrant workers. Liao said: "Farm produce is the major source of income for poor households and by finding markets for these products, the problems of low incomes could be solved."

Served by the government as a bridge, the operation team of Suning.

com's Chinese Specialty Pavilion Taishan Branch arrived at Qianfeng and purchased all the village's rice patches, which relieved villagers' worries about the future. He Hengqing, head of operations in the Taishan Branch said: "The problems of unsalable potatoes in Jiangmen in 2015 inspired us to launch the farm produce campaign with Suning.com and we sincerely hope that, combining with Taishan's poverty alleviation purposes and goals, we can change the embarrassing situations of agricultural products in poverty-stricken villages."

Taishan also launched an online "Poverty Alleviation APP" . The APP gathers most of the information about poor villages and households and carries out various targeted poverty alleviation activities. It breaks the traditional mode of assistance and a series of O2O low-cost mutual-assistance campaigns will be launched in this channel.

It is known that recently the first assistance activity on this APP was "The Love Basket" , which was put on the "Public Crowd funding" column. The high quality farm produce from 920 poor households were picked up and packaged as " Love 99 Happiness Basket" (the number 9 means permanence in China). There were altogether 1,000 baskets and 99 yuan for each. All the earnings were given back to poor households to ease their selling plight.

The "Path" for
Online Job Hunting at Hand

"Just use a pen and fill in the application form, then you can wait for job opportunities coming to you at home. This will spare you a lot of trouble." Recently, Lian Chengjian, a poor villager in Wanzhong, Hekou town just received a copy of this "Job Application Form". In fact, in order to promote targeted poverty alleviation, Xinxing county has introduced a real time human resource recruitment platform—Taoli Network Techonology Co., Ltd (abbreviated as "Taoli" below), which made the "online job application form" tailored to situations of poverty-stricken households.

Under the instructions of residential cadres, Lian Chengjian completed some resume questions such as personal information, work experience and employment intention. Lian told us that the cadres would upload his resume to Taoli platform to conduct job matching and that he could receive job information through mobile phones sent by the platform. He said: "Once successfully matched, I could accept an offer of employment."

Graduated from junior college, Lian Chengjian is a 22-year-old man worn out by "difficulties in job hunting". Compared with aimlessly submitting CVs on all kinds of recruitment websites, by having residential cadres input personal information and conducting real time job application through Taoli platform, villagers meet with less unnecessary problems and get more chances to be employed.

Lian Chengjian illustrated this point by citing an example: After his graduation, he sent over 100 copies of his resume on all job hunting websites and mobile software but were rebuffed again and again due to insufficient education background and lack of experience. And now he works in a Guangzhou-based company and with an intern salary of 2,300 yuan every month, he could have nothing left excluding daily expenses.

Lian says he hopes to find a better job through Taoli platform and his expected wage welfare is over 3,000 yuan. He told us: "If my monthly wage is more than 3,000 yuan, then I can send more money back home to get rid of the poor conditions as soon as possible."

According to overall inspection, by the end of June, there are 7,054 poverty-stricken households (16,681 people) in Xinxing county and to realize comprehensive poverty alleviation, the major issue is to solve the employment of 2446 households (9,569 people) with work labor and let them get rid of poverty by employment.

However, due to the restricting factors of geographical locations, transportation and backward information, poor households rely mainly on relatives' and friends' recommendations and it is fruitless for them to look for jobs in cities. Helping poverty-stricken households' employment has become the key point and difficulty of the three-year targeted poverty alleviation campaign. Xinxing introduces Taoli Network Technology Co., Ltd to help solve the employment issues of poor households. The Taoli platform adopts an "Internet + Labor employment" mode and operates in an O2O pattern facing all the archived household labor and send information of job positions to them through mobile phones. At the same time, poor households can also enhance their techniques by attending Taoli's vocational trainings so as to find better jobs and earn higher salaries.

The staff in Xinxing Poverty Alleviation Office Zhang Zhijun told us that in order to create more job opportunities, Xinxing and Taoli has signed a strategic cooperation contract with Taoli employment platform and the latter has set up Xinxing's targeted poverty relief project group. The two parties have conducted several researches on how to provide job descriptions and professional training for poverty-stricken households.

Considering that some poor villagers don't have smart phones, Taoli prepares and prints paper job application forms for them. In this way, households can either have residential cadres post their resumes on Taoli real time recruitment platform by submitting paper forms or conduct the process by themselves on the phones.

At present, Xinxing county is holding a "Labor Force Employment Poverty Alleviation Project" training and work advancement meeting, inviting the residential cadres and major secretaries from 15 major villages. By the end of this year, Taoli will provide several job positions for poor households, such as housekeeping job for women between 18 and 50, and positions for technicians, general workers, warehouse keepers, QA inspectors, welders and electricians.

High-speed Railways Have Changed the Lifestyles in Mountain Areas

High-speed Railways
Bring Popularity and Wealth

In the early summer, it is breezy and sunny in Guizhou. The tea growers are busy working in the green tea gardens as in previous years. And at the other end of the Guizhou-Guangdong high-speed railways, people are working speedily in front of computers to find market for the tea. This is a new change. With the development of technological information and transportation facilities, the tea growers in Guizhou and wholesalers in Guangdong are taking the "cloud" of Internet big data to enhance the credibility of Guizhou tea's quality safety and use the Internet to do big businesses. At the same time, with the opening of Guizhou-Guangdong high-speed railway and the integration into the three-hour economic circle in the Pearl River Delta, the trend of tea industry relieving poverty is rising.

Railway is the "artery" of the national economy. For years, besides ensuring people's convenient travelling, the railways have also played an important role in boosting economic development in poverty-stricken areas. In China, there is a sentence going like "Once the railway is opened, piles of gold could be got" . It shows railways' crucial role in connecting lines of the economic "arteries" around the nation.

Back in 1998, when the Guangzhou-Meizhou-Shantou railway was first opened, the counties along the road—Longchuan, Wuhua, Xingning and Fengshun were all "state-level poverty-stricken counties" , but by 2016,

▲ The opening of Wu-Guang high-speed railway.

all these counties had got rid of the old label. With the advancement of speed and performance of the Guangzhou-Meizhou -Shantou railroad and the gradual construction of Hui-Mei-Shan high-speed railway, the counties along the high-speed railway lines would face another good chance for development.

Simultaneously, there has been a "big industrial zone" in the areas along the Wuhan-Guangzhou railway opened in 2009. By now, the railway has been in operation for six years and the cities alongside the railway lines such as Shaoguan, Qingyuan and the ones along the Xiang- Er high-speed railway have undertaken over 10,000 projects transferred from the Pearl River Delta, with a total investment of over 500 billion yuan. In 2015, the GDP growth rates of cities like Qingyuan and Shaoguan, which are located along the high-speed railway, were all above 8% and the amount of increase was higher than those of any other cities in the province.

The "Zoo" on the Trains

In the past, the train connecting Guizhou and Guangdong took more than 18 hours to travel through 857 kilometers. The "slow trains" between Guizhou and Guangdong have been operating for almost half a century since the 19th century. Liu Wencheng, who often travelled by this train in the past remembered that many passengers would sit around in the last carriage of the train—the baggage car, with several pack baskets of live chickens piling up beside them. For the 61-year-old Liu Wencheng, he couldn't have been more familiar with this train line.

It was twenty years ago that he took this train to Guangdong to sell the tea leaves collected from the mountains in Guizhou. And twenty years later, he is still relying on this train to gain wealth. Every half a month, Liu and some of his friends will carry the tea leaves and walk for over an hour to catch the train heading for Guangdong by 13:01. The wholesale price for the tea is 20 yuan/jin and retail price 30. Deducting the fare, Liu can earn 500 yuan for one trip.

The several thousand yuan Liu earned from selling tea has become an important complement of his family incomes. With a sense of satisfaction about the convenience the railway has brought to her, Liu told us: "We can only earn money when there is convenient transportation and low ticket prices."

Twenty years ago, besides tea leaves, there were crowds of yelling ducks and geese and battling goats in the end of the carriages, which formed a scene of "zoo" . While people were talking with each other, a goose might lay an egg and caused wild laughters on the train.

Actually at that time, in order to facilitate Guizhou's minority villagers' traveling to trade fairs with cattle, some trains in Guangdong made specific "baggage carriage" to place cattle and large luggage and there were ladders for cattle to get on and off the trains. The "slow trains" for poverty alleviation here used to be an important "engine" to impel economic development in the regions along the road and improve people's living standards.

But now the "slow trains" have disappeared and the mission of the "baggage carriage" have ended. A high-speed railroad with an hourly speed of 350 kilometers is connecting Guizhou with Guangdong and the travelling time between the two provinces has shortened from 21 hours to 5 and a half.

In Hetaoba, Meitan county, Guizhou, 40 years of tea planting has relieved villagers from poverty and their life has changed from "living on brown rice and traveling over mountains for water" into "water is at hand and electricity-powered" . With the opening of Guizhou-Guangdong high-speed railway, villagers have built dams, tea gardens and roads and later established brands, associations and Internet sales. Just within a few years, the tea farmers, who used to live on weather, have targeted their visions at broader markets.

Jing Linbo is a Hetaoba villager who has been engaged in tea business for more than ten years. Besides owning a tea company, he also constructed a 6-unit tea-making workshop and is in charge of growing tea, purchasing and processing tea leaves.

However, the young man isn't satisfied with only doing a tea retailing and wholesaling business. Excluding costs, he can only earn a profit of 10 or 20 yuan per jin and the prospects for increasing profits are slim since prices are continually forced down by buyers. Jing Linbo believes that he needs to move from the bottom of the market and is determined to build his own brand. Ever since the Guizhou-Guangdong high-speed railway was opened, the costs for transportation has dramatically went down and as more people and products circulate in the area, tea farmers finally get rid of the trouble brought about by inconvenient traffic and Hetaoba village is beginning to step out of poverty.

Meitan county is a major tea-production area in Guizhou, and with a planting area of more than 500,000 units, the overall income of tea industry in 2014 reached over 3 billion yuan. As the origin of Meitan's tea industry and tea culture, Hetaoba village particularly "thrives on tea industry" . There are 10,000 units of tea gardens in the village, and 868 households are planting or processing tea. And the well-known Hetaoba tea leaves are purchased by tea dealers in large amount.

In 2014, the average income of local farmers reached 14,200 yuan per person, but more and more tea farmers are no longer satisfied to be the ring with lowest profits in the industrial chain. The Internet thus becomes a "powerful weapon" for tea growers to develop new markets. Since the end of 2014, Liu Shengyan, a tea grower, has been busy opening subscription accounts and service accounts to deliver news about "Yunxiang Tea" and let more people know about Xiangmei green tea by transmitting through beautiful words and pictures. Currently, dozens of corporations in Hetaoba have established their own online distribution channel on big E-commerce platforms such as TMALL and JD. COM and are making higher sales volume year by year.

How to convert tea-planting into an industry and change his own role from tea grower to tea dealer are questions Liu Zeyuan wants to answer. He is planning to unite with the leading tea-processing companies in the village to set up a tea "gathering company" . It aims at realizing no cutting-down of prices and no purchasing on credit in order to solve the problems of insufficient investment capitals and slow withdrawal of funds. At present, every year the county will have many tea growers and production enterprises take part in all kinds of domestic farm produce trade fair and tea exposition to let them find business opportunities.

Targeted Poverty Alleviation of High-speed Railways Free for Special Passengers

On 18 January, 2017, before Chinese Lunar New Year, four "Trains of Happiness" , leaving successively from Guangzhou and Shenzhen, took over 3,000 migrant workers back home to Guangxi, Guiyang, Hubei and Hunan.

Jishou in Hunan, Baise in Guangxi and Guiyang in Guizhou are all the poverty alleviation assistance areas of Guangdong. The K9064 train from Shenzhen to Jishou is a specialized line for the poverty alleviation campaign. Before passenger transport during the Spring Festival, Guangzhou Railway Group, with the help of the news media, sent out messages that Guangdong Human Resources and Social Security Office and benevolent enterprises would donate free train tickets for migrant workers from Jishou, Shibadong and the neighboring villages. The Group arranged railway conductors of Jishou origin to perform crew services and hold charity activities on the trains.

Liang Yongning, who took on crew services work, was a disable man, the initiator of the charitable organization "ComeBack Home Baby" and was rated as one of the ten most influential public figures in charity by Sina Weibo in 2016. He personally donated 10 train tickets to help the migrant workers from Shibadong go back home and celebrate the Spring Festival.

One among those who received a free ticket was a retired soldier called Duan Guangming. He is working in a electronics factory in Shenzhen and with a monthly salary of 5,000 yuan, his family's living standard is gradually improving.

The "motorcycle army" that needs to be taken care of every year. can also benefit from the convenience provided by the high-speed railways. As the restrictions of motors in Guangdong, Guangxi and Guizhou have become increasingly common, the high-speed rail accommodation power has increased by 20% in 2016 and could transfer 70,000 passengers every day. Therefore, on the basis of continuing to open specialized lines for motorcycle army, the benevolent high-speed railway opened in 2016 can bring more safety and convenience to the way home of "motorcycle army".

Characteristic Towns:
It's Nice Living in
Mountain Villages

Transition of the "Great Northern Wilderness" in Guangzhou

Lianma village, Lvtian, which is located in the northernmost of Guangzhou, borders on Xinfeng, Shaoguan in the north and Longmen, Huizhou in the east and is called as the "north door" of Guangzhou. In recent years, the fresh air and beautiful natural sceneries in Lianma has attracted attention to its tourism resources. And as Lianma being listed into Conghua district's "beautiful town" construction project, the village has taken on a new look and got rid of the old image of a poverty-stricken area. With the changes brought forth by the project, the lives in the mountains have become better and better. In the near future, living in mountains could become something the city dwellers dream about.

Lianma is Guangzhou's largest administrative village with 11 economic unions and a population of 1,406. The lands in Lianma are mainly in mountainous regions and due to the restrictions of geographical features, farmers can only grow produce such as "Sanhua Plum" and "sugar oranges" rather than regular vegetables. Pan Guangzao, party branch secretary of Lianma told us: "In the past, villagers made most of living on forest resources, but later the government issued strict policies to protect forests so the traditional mode of forest- oriented income system was broken. Villagers could only earn a slim income by charging for protecting

▲ The design of Lianma's ecological rainwater garden.

the water resources in protected forests, and much of capable work labor chose to work outside." As the village was remote and with a low living standard, it was regarded as the "Great Northern Wilderness" by locals in Conghua.

The embarassing situations in Lianma brought much concern to town and village cadres. How to effectively integrate and utilize current resources and find out a development model suitable for the village were the questions they want to answer. In the end of 2014, the leaders of Guangzhou made a survey about Lianma and pointed out its directions for developing ecological tourism, which brought new opportunities to the village. In 2015, Conghua district made the decision of converting Lianma into a "beautiful town" and this brought a "wind of change" to the village and gave out abundant fruit in a year's time. Since July 2013, Guangzhou has started three-year assistance to Lianma village, which brought a new appearance to it. In 2016, the collective income of Lianma has reached 565,300 yuan, with the 20 poor households earning an average annual income of 15,000 yuan, the place has turned into wealthy village .

The construction of "beautiful town" has brought breathtaking changes to Lianma and villagers suggest that the most evident ones are improved environment and increased incomes.

Since construction of infrastructure is the biggest livelihood project, the construction and improvement of Liansheng village exactly started with building facilities that benefit people. Pan Guangzao introduced to us that in the past year, Lianma gradually formed the construction scale of beautiful villages and there were great changes in the building of basic infrastructure, which included the expanding construction of roads, riverbanks, lanes, parking lots and sewage facilities. At present, a four-mile riverbank and 12-mile lane construction have already been completed and the 3.1-mile long social road linking G105 and Huangshakeng Economic Union has been asphalt-paved. In terms of environment, there are a lot of newly-added landscapes near the village committee, which brings the place a refreshing look.

From Farmers to
B&B Shopkeepers

Now a one-hour drive on the highway takes tourists directly from Guangzhou to Lianma and the gradual openings of highways have brought this northern mountainous village a lot of popularity and business opportunities. In September 2016, the college student's art hotel invested by Guangzhou Huaxia Vocational College announced its formal commencement for construction. The project was planned to last for three months, and with a total investment of 6 million yuan, it aimed at promoting local economic development by vitalizing spare farm houses to build modernized and ecological art bases.

Not far from the art hotel, some B&B accommodations are being built. The hotel called "Lanwu" standing right beside the village committee building is quite eye-catching. Walking into it, you can feel a natural sense of village life and the decorations are beautiful yet full of rural characteristics. This is the first B&B in Lianma, which was converted from the villager Chen Huichun's house.

Since the trial operation in the end of 2015, Chen's B&B has enjoyed great welcome from tourists. In the past, Chen was only an ordinary housewife and was responsible of planting vegetables and doing chores at home. But now, with the rapid development of "Lianma Town" , she has become a "shopkeeper" and earned a steady income.

The relative responsible officials in Lvtian town suggest that local government will choose 10 farm houses to build family stay as pilots and they will be operated in a "government + village collectivity + farm households" mode with a moderate support from fiscal capitals. These family stays will be uniformly managed by Guangzhou Beijingyuan Tourism Development Co., Ltd, which is a company established by the village and by doing so, irregular development and malicious competition between Lianma home stays can be avoided.

Besides B&Bs, the construction of peanut oil workshops and hotels designed by Guangzhou Art College painters which feature in urban agriculture and culture tourism is also under the way. Among these, Lianma Conference Center and Youth Hostel, which can accommodate 300 tourists, will be completed in 2017. At present, Chen Huichun is negotiating with other villagers to enlarge the management scope of farm stays and seize the business opportunities during the National Holiday. She is hopeful about the village's development: "In the future, more distinctive cultural and tourism facilities will be built in Lianma."

The northward ancient post road in Lianma is only left 300 meters long and the village committee has rebuilt it according to the few descriptions in the historical books. The village secretary Pan Guangzao hopes that the renovated road can "tell" the ancient stories in Lianma. The officials in Lvtian said: "Introducing projects doesn't mean earth-shaking removal and construction, it means sticking to the traditions and preserving the ecological distinctiveness of the town." Actually, right at the beginning of the construction, the village invited a team of China Rural Construction Institute to work out the plans of establishing a beautiful town, which focused on keeping rural characteristics.

Pan Guangzao told us: "Lianma tofu and peanut oil, as local special farm products, enjoy a high popularity and introducing corporations to upgrade farmers' production in industrial measures can not only enlarge production scale, but also demonstrate the traditional production arts." He also revealed that now the white spirit workshop had already invited masters in Wuliangye to teach the way of making liquor and refining the cultural values of brewage.

Conghua businessman Luo Ting has been looking for new investment opportunities for years and he came back to his hometown Lianma on the Spring Festival after leaving the place for more than a decade. With a sharp sense of business opportunities, he decided to return to his hometown and invest in urban agriculture. He said: "The construction in the town is in full swing and one can find opportunities everywhere." His first step is to renovate farm houses and invite designers to plan for farm stays and the second one is to develop green gardens by cooperating with villagers to plant and breed and develop urban agriculture with local characteristics. From traditional iron and steel trade to modern agriculture, Luo Ting has found a sticking point in Lianma to make the transformation from traditional capital to new business type. And by utilizing the advantaged ecological environment in Guangzhou, more and more investors like Luo Ting have drawn their capitals to the high-quality ecological resources of

Lianma. Currently, many corporations have settled in Lianma and the green farm produce from the origins of Liuxi River and the farmhouse cultural products will enter the Pearl River Delta.

Start-ups
Accelerate "Town" Construction

As the National Holiday approaches, Pan Anna, a post-80s girl, has to step up the purchase of goods in the neighboring areas in order to welcome the peak flow. After graduating from college in 2006, Pan used to work in the town government. In the end of 2015, she chose to settle in Lianma and established her first entrepreneurship project— "Beiyuan Home".

"Bei means the northernmost of Guangzhou and Yuan means the origin of Liuxi River. We wish to make our customers feel at home." With a little investment, Pan Anna started with vitalizing adobe houses and renovated farm houses by decoration and repairment.

Since the end of 2015, "Beiyuan Home" has gained some popularity on the Internet and tourists have gained deeper impression of Lianma through its accommodation and services. Pan Anna told us as a small business start-up, she invested monthly profits to the hotel and infrastructure construction such as adding fences for streams and paving black bricks to gradually improve the neighboring environment.

Ecological tourism and modern agriculture add vitality to rural industries and the development opportunities brought by green economy have attracted many young people to come back to Lianma. Pan Guangzao said: "Learning that the development of specialized town is under way, more and more youngsters come to the village for opportunities and these include young villagers, students and some start-ups." He also told us that dozens of migrant workers had come back to the village and the change in demographic structure had added vitality to this mountainous village and the construction was accelerating.

Not all reforms could go smoothly. As for the changes in Lianma, villagers' incomprehension stems from unfamiliarity and their support stems from the feelings about the benefits brought by changes. Pan Guangzao said that the development orientation for Lianma was to build an ecological scenic spot. Therefore, constructing B&Bs, home-stays and village hotels will be one of the most important projects for Lianma from now on. With the influential power brought by advertisement, the quiet and clear natural environment in Lianma has attracted many tourists to come. Pan introduced to us: "At present, we have already opened three home-stays and once at weekends or on public holidays, swarms of tourists will come for specialized dishes and live here for some days. Since the Spring Festival, one shop has earned 100,000 yuan." In January 2016, the DaGuang highway was opened, which brought significant influence on Lianma. Under the efforts of committee cadres, the name of "Lianma" was added on the board of the exit of DaGuang highway, greatly adding the popularity of Lianma. Driving off from Lianma exit, one could arrive at the village with only a five-mile national road drive. Now it takes only 80 minutes to drive from Guangzhou central districts to Lianma, which is very fast and convenient. On the May Day Holiday in 2016, the home- stays in Lianma was filled with tourists and the supply was unable to meet the demand.

In order to encourage villagers to support the development of construction and increase their initiatives for starting up their own business, the village committee also issued preferential policies to offer the top 10 households who took the lead in building B&Bs and home-stays a 50,000 yuan grant. At present, among all the projects in Lianma, when it relates to human resources and mechanical equipment, villagers will be firstly considered under the same conditions so as to increase their employment opportunities and incomes.

The Characteristic Town in Conghua Has Become the "New Engine" of Regional Innovation

On the last weekend of November 2016, the First Guangzhou Straw Festival was held in Xitang village. The theme of it was not only ecological tourism and leisure sightseeing but also the beginning of adding comic elements to the core districts of fairy tale town, which was the first cooperation of Animation Association and Xitang fairy tale town. Earlier these days the concerned department of the General Administration of Sports have officially signed a cooperation agreement of building a "national outdoor industry demonstration zone" with Conghua district. In the next five years, some big events and activities such as Guangzhou Camping Festival, Outdoor Activity Festival and National Mountaineering and Fitness Convention will be held in the characteristic town. Under the attraction of brand activities, streams of people, information and capitals from all over the country will connect with Conghua.

After the autumn harvest, Xitang village is covered with golden paddy fields. In the end of every November, the locals make the straws into simple scarecrows for entertainment. In 2016 the Straw Festival was upgraded into a urban-scale activity, which attracted enormous crowds of people and business opportunities.

Xitang is located in the northeast of Aotou town and is beside the

S355 line. The village, which is approximately 4.2 square meters large, is 11 miles away from downtown Conghua in the east and 60 miles away from Guangzhou in the south and has a farm land of 1,998 units. In the past, the development in Xitang was extremely backward and most young man chose to work outside.

In the end of 2015, Xitang was listed into the Conghua's construction of characteristic town and defined as "fairy tale town". How to make this into reality? The related official in Aotou town told us: "The first step is to implement infrastructure construction and environment improvement, the second is to insert endogenous dynamics to development by introducing different corporations and lastly is to settle in comic elements and resources."

Chen Haitao, village secretary of Xitang told us: "Xitang is affluent in ecological resources and it is the locals' sincere hope to get through the channel from ecology to industries and bring vitality for rural development." In the beginning of 2016, Xitang gradually introduced three urbanized agriculture corporations and several months ago, some villagers began to return to the village for job opportunities and the once deserted village was alive again. Thirty local villagers became greenhouse workers and they need to take good care of vegetables and pack the vegetables into different family packages according to their requirements and eventually deliver these packages by cold chain to 200 households in Guangzhou.

"The actual aim of the Straw Festival is to earn popularity for the town and introduce more corporations to development a fairy tale tourism town centering on 'three rural issues' by melting with animation culture." The related officials in Conghua revealed the "ambition" of the Straw Festival to us.

In 2016 the construction of 19 characteristic towns in Xitang has already entered the implementation stage. After the Straw Festival, Xitang will welcome a new round of reconstruction and will integrate resources to build some ecological science popularization bases such as "Seedling Kingdom" and "Insect Kingdom" to provide places for sketch and inspiration-stimuli for animation corporations.

Baoqu Rose World, Sakura Garden, Blossom Garden and several ecological tourism scenic spots decorate Xihe village with splendid seas of flowers and make it look like an amorous painting. With the impulsion of characteristic town project, the local government actively encouraged land circulation, which attracted several enterprises to settle in. The official in Xihe said that the local's agricultural production structure with high production and high added-value had realized the industrialization of flower production and enhanced the planting benefits. At present, 35 enterprises have settled in Xihe and as more than 10,000 units of land are already put into production, a flower production and sight-seeing industry featuring in producing fresh cut flowers, orchids, potted flowers, sakuras and characteristic seedlings have initially taken shape.

The official on Conghua suburban streets told us: "We plan to build Xihe into the most exotic town in Guangzhou and construct the only distinctive agricultural park in Guangdong here." From Lvtian in the north to the southern suburbs, several characteristic towns have preliminarily formed and taken on a different look.

By now, Conghua has built several characteristic towns according to the results of research. These include: the northernmost Lianma town featuring in camping and excursion, the southern amorous Xihe town built on flower resources, the Wenquan wealth town comprising characteristic finance, start-up innovation and romantic wedding and the Xitang fairy tale town targeting at children and parenting market.

Establishing Hundreds of Provincial Characteristic Towns in Guangdong by 2020

Characteristic towns mean the new development zones in the specified areas in cities and towns which integrate specialized industries and blend the functions of business, culture, tourism and living.

Focusing on distinctive leading industries and traditional industries, Guangdong will build nine characteristic towns. These towns will emphasize "character" and while keeping the industries distinctive, the patterns of the towns should also be distinctive.

In the meantime, the characteristic towns should also promote innovative entrepreneurship. In Zhejiang, where the promotion of distinctive towns is under way, the outcomes of effective investment and consumer enthusiasm have emerged. Taking Songshan Lake, Dongguan as an example, the local government is striving to build an "Internet+" town and actively improving the innovative start-up ecology by combining its industrial characteristics. And now the distinctive Internet industrial cluster has taken shape. The town aims at building a 2.2 million square meter start-up base and fostering 3-5 leading enterprises and 500 innovative small and medium-sized corporations in the Internet industry by 2018.

廣東最窮村莊
扶貧記：
與石灰岩地貌
的鬥爭

石灰岩山村的守望者

在電影《火星救援》裡，在孤獨的火星種著土豆的馬特·蒙達面對的條件是極端艱苦。但至少他還有肥沃的火星土壤，為他孕育一季又一季的土豆。在孟山村，雖然不缺空氣，可土壤、水等必需品卻是稀罕物。

廣東有石灰岩山區六千二百零八平方公里，占全省面積的百分之三點五，主要分佈在粵北和粵西地區，粵東北有零星出現。這些地區有一個共同的特點，大部分都是廣東最為貧困的地區。黎埠鎮孟山村位於廣東省北部的陽山縣，屬典型的石灰岩山區，山多地少，同時嚴重缺水，平均海拔五百多米。七年前，駐村扶貧組進駐時的統計顯示，全村三百七十八戶中，有貧困戶一百二十七戶四百三十七人，低保五保六十九戶一百七十一人。

孟山村為什麼這麼貧窮？我們先來看看孟山村的自然條件。作為山區，農民最重視的自然是土地。孟山村的田地全部分佈在石灰岩土質的山坡上。石灰岩山區的典型地貌，帶給這裡的影響十分深刻。在孟山村，「石山」和「土山」的交錯分佈中，被切割得分散的小地塊，幾乎產不出經濟效益。沒有礦山，沒有工廠，又無力改變自然，孟山村民在自然經濟的脆弱中日復一日地艱難活著。

很多村民自己也難以用語言描述清楚自己家田地的位置和樣子。當地最經典的自嘲式笑話是，有一天下雨，一農戶披著斗笠上山耕地，到了地裡，雨停了，農戶將斗笠隨手丟在了地上，然後一塊塊為自家土地翻土。可忙了一天，農戶發現自家的土地少了一塊。農戶找了半天也沒找到，臨近傍晚，農戶起身收行裝準備回家。結果當他拿起斗笠的時候發現，斗笠下有一塊小小地田，正是他剛剛漏掉的那塊地。笑話有些誇張，可卻反映出孟山村村民的尷尬。

其實這種尷尬在石灰岩地貌的山區十分常見。雖然地理面積大，但可利用的耕地面積卻少得可憐。零星分佈的耕地導致大面積種植以及工業化種植手段都無法應用在農作上。就算有一些能夠耕種的土地，耕種的農作物也受到限制，高產值的農作物基本難以種植，只能種植木薯、玉米等農作物。

惡劣的環境還伴隨著基礎設施建設的極度匱乏。孟山村四百四十畝水田中有二百八十五畝是「望天田」。用村委會主任陳金勝的話說，全年只能耕種一造，無法灌溉耕作。「眼看著天上下來雨水，卻留不住。」

解決「望天田」，建設水利設施實現灌溉，村民們在扶貧幫扶組來之前，其實做夢都在想挖幾口水塘，以解決農業灌溉和飲水問題。早在二十一世紀初，村民們曾經從深山挖了一條細溝，將石頭縫裡滲出的山泉水引到了山下。可由於財力有限，山泉水引下來後只流進了幾口深約二米的蓄水池，等村民們用水管將蓄水池的水引到自家門口時，已經水量不多，滲不出幾滴水了。

而要解決全村的飲用水問題必須挖塘打井，需要投資二十萬元，可讓人尷尬不已的是，當時整個村子的村民經濟收入主要靠外出打 工及村民種植油茶零散作物，人均年收入僅為三千元，平時生活捉襟見肘，更不要說拿出多餘的錢集資修建水利工程。

隨著全球變暖，厄爾尼諾現象增強，世界銀行曾作出警示會有一億人因厄爾尼諾現象致貧。這一億人就包括廣東高海拔地區石灰岩山區的村民。

村民在石灰岩山區生活靠天吃飯，如果遇上雨雪旱澇等災情，就更加毫無抵抗能力。村子裡稍有能力的人，慢慢都選擇搬遷了。在二〇一三年前，孟山村一些村民小組，沒有一棟新房，多數村民家都是建於上世紀三〇年代到五〇年代間的土坯房，土坯房外牆上還留著上世紀六〇年代的宣傳標語。

▌「突圍者」回不去的故鄉

　　二〇一六年中國的流動人口大軍總數達到了二點四五億。流動人口是在中國戶籍制度條件下的一個概念，指離開了戶籍所在地到其他地方居住的人口，國際上，類似的群體被稱為「國內移民」。中國流動人口的規模在改革開放後的三十多年中持續增長，尤其是二十世紀九〇年代以後增長速度明顯加快，從一九八二年的六百五十七萬人增長到二〇一〇年的二點二億人，達到了前所未有的規模，占全國總人口的百分之十七左右。北京、上海和廣州等城市的當地常住居民中，約百分之四十是流動人口。大部分流動人口是從農村流動到城市的年輕勞動力。

　　流動人口中有一部分人是看中大城市的機會，另一部分人則是因為家鄉惡劣的生存環境而被迫背井離鄉。如果人們在七年前來到清遠市的一些大山貧困區會發現，沿著村路一路東行，村子裡寂靜無聲，兩邊的房屋老舊殘破，一些屋子呈現傾頹之勢。村裡大部分村民能走的都走了，留下來的都是老人和小孩，還有的是需要照顧老人沒法出去打工的人。

　　這些山村在上一個十年中沒有變化嗎？其實幾年前孟山村也有變化。在孟山村大部分村民眼中，近十年來，孟山村的變化僅限於：修通了一條砂石路和一棟兩層的村委會辦公樓。一九九七年，村民們湊了兩萬多塊錢，終於打通了通往竹田、水塘等小組的砂石路。而建於一九九九年的村委會小樓，過了好幾年，才找到孟山籍外出人員和扶貧單位贊助，還清建樓債務。

在先天貧瘠的地理條件和日漸頻繁的天災的雙重擠壓下，村裡有能力者慢慢選擇了遷移和流動來進行突圍。可是突圍並不順利，外遷者大多無一技之長，想生存、發展、穩定也不容易，由於入戶難，還遇到子女教育、就業、計畫生育管理等一系列社會問題。

　　上世紀九〇年代，村裡人第一次集體走出大山，去佛山順德做拆樓工人。集體出走並沒讓村裡人賺到財富，加之不習慣大山外面的生活，大部分壯勞力又回到了孟山村。六十七歲的熊火蘭走了一條完全不同的道路。當時他沒去做拆樓工人。他到鄰近的連州撿垃圾謀生。熊火蘭撿垃圾的工作和很多巴西貧民窟裡垃圾回收工作一樣。當時中國主要城市並未建立垃圾分類系統，這些拾荒者們把整個城市的垃圾撿回來，把垃圾裡有用的可回收再利用材料分揀出來，進行二次變賣，讓這些可回收再利用資源得到充分應用。踏實肯幹，熊火蘭在五十多歲的時候討到了老婆。在整個孟山村，像熊火蘭這樣在外打工賺到一點錢就搬遷的村民，在二十一世紀頭十年慢慢多了。二〇〇〇年十二月份，孟山村全村人口一千九百四十四人，到二〇〇九年底這一數字是一千八百二十三人，除去少數死亡人口，人口減少基本是由於人口外遷。

　　可是外遷也不是一勞永逸，對這些外遷人口而言，面臨的問題仍然存在，在由農村人向城市人的轉變過程中，想要保證生存發展的持續穩定性並不容易。因為他們大多無一技之長。

扶貧就是讓留守者堅定信心

石灰岩山區之窮是廣東山區扶貧工作存在已久的困局。對類似孟山村這樣的石灰岩山區而言，其本身生產資源極度匱乏，生存條件又極為惡劣，政府即便花費大力氣在此採取一些開髮型脫貧措施，其發揮的作用也十分有限。

從一九九七年開始，當地對石灰岩山區進行了一系列的幫扶工作，比如發放種植、養殖基金，幫助當地農戶解決缺少資金投入生產等問題。但由於一些技術、銷售困難的原因，最後「生產資金」大多成了「生活資金」，並未有效扭轉當地的貧困態勢。

如何盤活當地經濟也是一門大學問。滿山遍野的油茶樹鬱鬱蔥蔥、潔白亮麗的茶花散發著淡淡的清香……這是孟山村現在的新面貌。自二○○九年初起，廣東電網清遠供電局、陽山縣供銷社出手，與黎埠鎮孟山村結成幫扶夥伴，採取幫扶措施，在三年時間使該村一百二十七戶貧困戶基本實現脫貧。

當地村民細數了油茶前景，一畝可以種一百二十株左右，每畝油茶年產油約兩百斤，即使按照二十元／斤來算，一年就可以收入四千元。目前孟山村油茶種植面積大概有四百畝左右，每戶貧困戶的種植規模分別在二到五畝不等。

油茶的掛果期需要三至五年，十年以後將進入盛果期，穩產收穫期可達到八十年以上。五十四歲的朱才英是家中唯一的勞動力，兒子成年卻患上精神疾病；八年前老伴患癌症去世，十萬多元的積蓄全部清空。「家裡二畝多山地都轉租給種植油茶的人，我收了租金還能為他們打工，隨著油茶掛果越來越多，以後的收入會更高。」朱才英說。

金融手段助力最貧困山村

　　幫扶組帶來了產業脫貧，也帶來了金融扶貧。金融手段的創新也改變了廣東貧困村的落後面貌。陽山縣創造性地提出「扶貧經紀人」（自願幫扶貧困戶的村幹部、能人大戶）的概念。駐村幹部物色為人勤奮老實、脫貧願望強烈的貧困戶，並讓他們與能人大戶結對。陽山扶貧辦通過借款扶持「扶貧經紀人」擴大生產，再通過「扶貧經紀人」捆綁幫扶貧困戶。

　　最重要的是，陽山縣扶貧辦為每個村莊在銀行墊資十萬元撬動五十萬元借款，由「扶貧經紀人」擔保借款給貧困戶。正是通過這樣的金融創新，孟山村裡竟然出現了好幾個大型養殖基地。

　　村民面臨著資金短缺的難題。為了幫孟山村籌集資金，幫扶單位創新性地設立了村級互助資金。

　　「村級互助資金就可以說是『村級銀行』。」據陽山縣扶貧開發辦公室主任潘志偉介紹，村級互助資金主要由政府籌集，目前，政府已經為孟山村籌集了近四十萬元，貧困戶無須存款，就可以借三千元。

　　「如果與龍頭企業合作，還可以向農行申請不超過互助金五倍的借款。」潘志偉舉例說，如一個貧困戶最多可以借九千元，那麼，他就可以向農行申請四點五萬元的貸款。

　　當然，貧困戶也並非可以隨意到村級自助組織借款，需要大戶擔保，或者三戶以上提供擔保。「村級銀行」打動了村民發展的心。村民江思文說，做一個豬舍、養三百多頭豬需要十萬元。如果只靠自己，很難拿出那麼多資金。而通過村級互助資金，自己終於可以貸款幾萬元，「我的目標是做達到千頭豬規模的養豬場」。

▌棄貧：整體搬遷迎來新生

廣東粵北山區是廣東較早探索移民搬遷的地區。針對石灰岩地區特殊的地理環境和惡劣的生產生活條件，近十多年來，當地一直在通過有效的搬遷移民進行扶貧。當地比較成功的做法是，將搬遷人口遷移至劃定的區域，並幫助搬遷人口尋找工作，解決子女上學問題。居民搬遷後，人均純收入普遍提高，並基本融入安置地的生活。

韶關乳源瑤族自治縣大橋鎮中沖村地處深山，進出不易，一路上從高速轉入國道，國道駛進鄉間公路，公路變小路，最後才走進鄉村。

這裡是廣東少數幾個冬天下雪的地方，每年十一月份之後，山上一片枯黃。雖說都是地處嶺南，然而與溫暖濕潤的珠三角地區相比，這是一片沉睡的鄉村。

如今這裡的面貌和以前卻大不相同，半山腰上的瑤族新村是中沖村村民整體搬遷出來建設的，從深山之中搬到縣城的邊沿，離縣城只有三公里的距離，村口就是修建不久的環山公路，出入非常方便。

這次搬遷改變了村民的出行習慣，如果是二○一○年前，趙天香要想去一趟城裡都是一件大事。他雞鳴時分就得出發，走上四個小時的山路，到了縣城，趕快置辦完貨品，就得馬上回程。否則天黑以後，山路狹窄，懸崖陡峭，非常危險。

中沖村整體重建後，孩子可以進入縣城的小學讀書。新村是瑤族風格，每個村民的家有兩層小樓，一百三十平方米，白牆青瓦紅欄杆，繪上瑤族的古老紋飾。離開深山，村民多了幾條活路，現在可以務農，也可以務工。

二〇一〇年開始，中沖村開始種植高山蔬菜。現在全村有三個基地，即蔬菜、油茶和黃煙基地，其中高山蔬菜已經成為廣東的一個品牌，種植的茄子、辣椒、豆角供應廣州、深圳、東莞等地，中沖村所在的大橋鎮已經成了珠三角的菜籃子。

中沖村只是廣東貧困山區移民整體搬遷的一個縮影。早在上世紀九〇年代，廣東就開始了龐大的移民整體搬遷工程。一九九四至一九九七年，就有十萬清遠山區貧困村民實現了整體搬遷。二〇一一至二〇一六年又有三十萬廣東山區貧困農民異地搬遷。農民搬遷後，政府幫忙建設新房和配套措施，農民得以直接從自然條件惡劣的地區搬入經濟較發達地區，享受當地的公共服務。

在最新出台的廣東省扶貧政策中，有八大扶貧工程，其中之一就是要通過改善人居環境，鞏固易地移民搬遷成果，支持安置區配套公共設施建設和遷出區生態修復；對不具備生產生活條件的零散分佈的貧困戶，實施插花搬遷；對沒有搬遷意願的少數貧困戶，探索以生態補償方式讓其中有勞動能力的就地轉化為護林員等生態保護人員。

教育扶貧：
扶貧先扶智

雷州的「撒哈拉沙漠」

中國大陸最南端的雷州半島，西臨北部灣，東涉南海，南隔十八海里的瓊州海峽與海南島相望。五千到六千年前，雷州半島這塊紅土地上，已有人類活動，秦時納入華夏版圖，古合浦郡治所在地。是漢王朝對外貿易重要基地，史稱「海上絲綢之路」始發港。唐代後，李氏皇朝才有計畫「閩民於合州」（唐貞觀八年改合州為雷州）。宋以後南遷漢人（主要為閩南人居多）逐年遞增，加速了雷州半島之開發步伐。千百年生生息的半島人，創造了很多獨特的非物質文化。雷州歌作為用雷州半島的獨特語言雷語方言演唱的歌曲是國家級非物質文化遺產。雷州半島的獨特語言與南粵大地，特別是經濟富裕的珠三角地區的廣府方言有很大區別。

位於粵西雷州半島地區有一個東塘村，村裡有一個走不出的怪圈，改革開放這麼多年來，無論走出去多少打工的青壯年，都無法留在當地安心打工，到頭來，全部都要回到這個全省聞名的貧困村裡。

根據二〇一〇年統計，東塘村共有九百零八戶三千九百五十七人，處於貧困線以下的有四百六十八戶二千零二十一人，貧困率超過百分之五十一。按世界銀行統計，三十年前中國的整體貧困率約為百分之五十三。也就是說，這裡的生活水平還停留在上世紀八〇年代。

在這片貧瘠的土地上，村支書王南幹了整整十三年。直到二〇一〇年，他才在兩個弟弟的幫助下，告別茅草屋，蓋上紅磚房。

貧困，為什麼會一直在這個小村莊停留衍生？扶貧又是怎麼讓貧困脫離這片土地？

　　撒哈拉沙漠是世界上除南極洲之外最大的荒漠，撒哈拉沙漠位於非洲北部，北到地中海，南到蘇丹草原。位於阿特拉斯山脈和地中海（約北緯 35°線）以南，約北緯 14°線（250 毫米等雨量線）以北。撒哈拉沙漠約形成於二百五十萬年前，是世界僅次於南極洲的第二大荒漠，也是世界最大的沙質荒漠，是地球上最不適合生物生存的地方之一。其總面積約容得下整個美國本土。而位於廣東雷州半島的東塘村常被人稱為雷州的「撒哈拉沙漠」。

　　東塘村的自然稟賦可以用「惡劣」兩個字來形容。土地貧瘠，嚴重沙化。雨季時，海風長驅直入，帶來豐沛降水，田裡的積水半年也排不完；但這裡也會一連好幾個月滴雨未下，村民只能眼睜睜看著禾苗乾死。

　　進入二十一世紀，中國加大了對農業的投入力度，國家糧食收購價格節節攀升，廣東稻穀每斤最低收購價逼近一元。但這一切，在二〇一二年前和東塘人似乎無關，好的年頭，種的糧食僅僅夠填飽肚子。靠田吃飯的東塘村民，實際是靠天吃飯。即使是最好的年頭，畝產至多也就五百斤。而在其他地區，依靠機械科學種植，畝產千斤早已不稀奇。可是東塘村的村民大多只上過小學和初中，不少人連科學種田「聽都沒聽過」。在東塘，機械化種植幾乎是空白，拖拉機、肥料這些新東西，在缺乏文化技術知識的大多村民眼裡實在多餘，既不會搗鼓也不想用。

　　二〇一〇年以前，村民黎學貴的房子裡家徒四壁，沒有日曆，沒有時鐘。幾乎是文盲的黎學貴，這樣的生活延續多年。早晨他跟著鄰居下地，晚上跟著大家收工。家裡的三個孩子成為黎學貴的負擔。可自家的土地卻沒有多少，為了提高產出，黎學貴只能一地兩用，割完水稻後，立刻種上蕃薯。曾經有技術員告訴村民，應該如何科學施種才能提高產量，但他和鄰居卻怎麼也記不住，更學不會。

　　週末，兩個讀書的孩子必須回家，因為田裡需要他們，但家裡卻沒有多餘的床，兩個孩子只能去鄰居家借住。然而就是這樣耗盡心力地去維護這一畝三分田，耗時耗力，甚至包括對生活的熱情，都花費在這裡。因為，這裡能讓一家人吃上飯，遇上好的年頭甚至可以吃飽飯。不幸的是，幾乎沒有家庭能從口糧中省出可供變現的餘糧。有人曾試著種花生、辣椒，但都「只有熱情，不懂技術」，忙活了一年甚至還要賠錢。

無法融入的外鄉世界

上世紀九〇年代，數以百萬計的務工人員湧入珠三角，這個遍地是金的尋夢天堂。

東塘人也加入了務工大軍。滾滾車輪，載著一批批懷有賺錢養家夢的人走出東塘。然而，幸運之神似乎有意躲著他們——村民從未聽說誰在外面賺了錢，走出去的人很快又都回到村裡。

十多年過去了，除了通向村裡的黃土路鋪上了水泥，村民說其他沒有任何改變。

東塘村鄭鑫一家，四年前買的紅磚，現在還堆在角落，早已佈滿青苔。二〇〇六年，鄭家住了幾十年的茅草屋已破敗不堪。外面下雨，屋裡漲大水。這年的一場大雨後，茅屋遭遇滅頂之災，坍塌了大半。

就在同一年，鄭鑫二十二歲的兒子初三畢業，在朋友介紹下去了廣州打工。一家人認為老大去了大城市闖，生活就有了依靠，於是決定蓋房。從親戚那裡借的二萬蓋房錢很快就花完了，但在廣州的兒子卻連飯都吃不飽。因為聽不懂普通話，更不懂技術，他只好跟著老鄉撿破爛。蓋房夢被迫中斷，原來的草房亦不復存在。無奈之下，他們搬進附近的樹林，用樹枝搭起兩個「木帳篷」。小的給老母親住，鄭鑫和老婆住在大帳篷裡。工作了四年的鄭家老大，現在每個月工資僅八百元。在電話裡，他告訴奶奶，外面太苦，他想回家種田。

村裡的中年人，年輕時也和鄭家老大一樣，曾走出東塘，到珠三角或鄰近省份打工，但頂多做三年就回來了。究其原因還是東塘人文化程度不高，一口地道的「雷州普通話」，濃重的鄉音讓人難以理解。溝通不暢自然也消磨了晉陞的通道。

滿口的「雷普」（雷州普通話）源自東塘小學。當年的學校課堂上，老師用一字一頓的普通話教孩子學拼音，轉身喝道：「安靜！」此時，普通話又變成雷州方言。這是二〇一〇年以前的景象，當時三百零一名學生全部來自本村，老師也都是本地人，他們也無奈，村裡有電視的家庭不超過二十分之一，互聯網更是新鮮事物，土生土長的老師很少接觸到外面的世界。

很多教師是小學畢業後就留校任教，教書多年後通過進修才拿到文憑，早就錯過了學普通話的最佳時期。「雷州普通話」就這樣代代相傳。表面上看，東塘「小升初」的入學率達到百分之百。農村孩子上學晚，八歲上一年級「還算早」，進入初中時大部分都超過十六歲。

一批批說著純正「雷州普通話」的大齡初中生，走出家門，重拾父輩之路。現實再多的困難，也阻擋不住他們對外面世界的渴望。一批批走出去的東塘人，在外艱難闖蕩一兩年後，含淚而歸。接過父輩的鋤頭，結婚生子，終其貧窮而平凡的一生。

「中國製造二〇二五」 與教育扶貧

二〇一四年十二月，「中國製造二〇二五」這一概念被首次提出。四個月後，二〇一五年三月五日，李克強在全國兩會上作《政府工作報告》時首次提出「中國製造二〇二五」的宏大計畫。「中國製造二〇二五」是中國政府實施製造強國戰略第一個十年的行動綱領。第一步，到二〇二五年邁入製造強國行列；第二步，到二〇三五年中國製造業整體達到世界製造強國陣營中等水平；第三步，到新中國成立一百年時，綜合實力進入世界製造強國前列。

「中國製造二〇二五」這樣的製造業大升級任務要完成，優質的職業人才教育是不可或缺的。隨著城市化進程推進，廣東大量流動人口就有成為優質產業工人的潛力，珠三角中國製造業兩大門戶地區，需要大量優質產業工人。可貧困阻擋了山區流動人口學習知識、培訓技能的道路。東塘村的教育現狀也反映了廣東教育扶貧的難題：教育基礎設施建設投入不足，師資力量不均衡，畢業生出路不明朗。

對於這些貧困家庭和他們的孩子，接濟衣物、糧食和解決住房等，也許能果腹暖身，但只是除一時之困，並非長 久之計。扶貧須先扶智。大山裡的居民其實知道，要想富，得走出去；要想走出去，要多讀幾年書。學好普通話，提高文化素質，才能在「人」這個問題上確保扶貧效果。

二〇〇九年十二月，深圳坪山新區與包括東塘村在內的東里鎮四村結成幫扶夥伴。不懂普通話，職業技能無法提高？東塘村貧困戶中有勞動力一百九十八人，深圳坪山新區按照「培訓一人、就業一人、脫貧一戶」的原則，安排他們免費參加技能培訓，有組織、有目的地引導其到新區務工，努力掌握技術和經驗，為未來回鄉創業推進集體脫貧做準備。

與此同時，村道一旁的東塘小學變了模樣，坪山新區投入三點三六萬元建設的一棟鋼筋混凝土結構的公廁赫然挺立在東塘小學的西南角，同期建設的還有一座垃圾池，徹底解決了該校三百多名師生入廁難的問題，顯著地改善了學校的衛生環境。

在村外，有陌生人偶遇幾個騎車嬉鬧的村裡小孩兒，原以為他們就像一路上遇到的大人們一樣，聽不懂普通話。豈料，突然一個小男孩用普通話上前問道：「你要去哪兒？」

治貧先治愚

二〇一五年十月十六日，在二〇一五減貧與發展高層論壇上，來自廣東順德的碧桂園創始人楊國強被授予「中國消除貧困獎（創新獎）」，他開啟了教育扶貧領域「政社互動」幫扶的範本。作為地產大亨，楊國強和他的女兒楊惠妍曾登頂「福布斯」中國財富富豪榜，改革開放將近四十年，碧桂園從無到有，地產項目遍布中國一、二、三線城市。

二〇一〇年以來，楊國強父女和碧桂園六年間捐贈超過十三億元用於廣東扶貧濟困事業。此前捐贈的超八億元，用於在清遠、肇慶、廣州等地推進樹山村綠色產業扶貧、懷集縣扶貧、梯面鎮扶貧、送技術技能下鄉培訓、廣東碧桂園職業學院、滴灌精準扶貧等六大項目。

出生於廣東順德一個貧困農民家庭的楊國強，十七歲前幾乎沒穿過鞋。他從不曾忘記，在他因家貧不得不輟學之際，政府不僅免了他每學期七元學費，還給予二元助學金，讓他完成了高中學業。他深切感受到教育對於徹底脫貧的積極意義，事業有成後，他開始踏上教育扶貧之路。

多年以後，當他回憶起年少奮鬥的時光時，覺得那應該 是追求知識的渴望。楊國強說，在碧桂園集團的財務總監，是他同宗族的兄弟，兩人同時得了國家二元錢補貼，免了七元錢學費。兩人用四元錢去廢品收購站買了一堆書，甚至包括大學課本。

一九九七年，楊國強捐資一百萬元匿名設立「仲明獎學金」資助貧困大學生，十八年中不斷增加捐助，先後有八千多名學子受惠；二〇〇二年，楊國強出資二點六億元創辦了國華紀念中學，免費招收家庭貧困、成績優秀的學生，提供助學金直至學生完成大學、碩士、博士所有階段的學業；二〇一三年，楊國強又出資三點五億元創辦廣東碧桂園職業學院，所有入讀學生不僅免除一切費用，還領取日常生活補貼。廣東碧桂園職業學院現在是廣東典型的職業教育扶貧項目。

目前，這所全免費的大專學校，接收了六百七十二名貧困學生。經過兩年招生，其中大部分為廣東籍貧困學生。

二〇一二年，在清遠市佛岡縣水頭鎮，楊國強探索出了另外一種教育扶貧方式，他將職業教育的課堂搬到了村子裡，開展「送技術技能下鄉培訓項目」。該項目對全鎮十六到六十週歲適齡勞動力，開展免費的技術技能培訓，還聯繫用工單位，幫助受訓農民找工作。三年來，該項目免費培訓一萬六千四百六十九人，其中八千一百五十人取得叉車、電工、家政育嬰師等九種職業資格證書，通過推薦就業，三千八百二十八人進城就業。

楊國強認為，學院一方面要系統培養高素質技術技能型人才；另一方面要以學院的菁英式培養來改變社會對高職的看法，從而讓更多學子喜歡讀高職，進而改良中國高等教育結構。

來自人社部的一項統計也驗證了楊國強的說法，中國二點二五億第二產業就業人員中，技能勞動者總量僅為一點一九億人，僅製造業高級技工一項的缺口就高達四百餘萬人，高級技能人才的供需矛盾十分嚴重，從而阻礙了企業的技術升級。二〇一五年「兩會」上，身為全國政127協委員的楊國強聯合三位全國政協委員，提交了一份《關於鼓勵和引導民營企業積極參與教育扶貧的提案》。

　　重視職教扶貧這一思路得到了國家層面的認可。國務院發布規定，對構建現代職業教育體系提出了明確的目標要求。

　　教育扶貧投入大、環節多、時間長，堅持不易，但效果顯著，可以做到「培養一人，脫貧一戶」，徹底阻斷貧困代際傳遞，實現個人、家庭、社會的共贏。十八年的教育扶貧，四萬多名受助者擺脫了貧困，楊國強說：「我所擁有的財富只是社會交給我保管的，有了能力幫助別人是很自然和正常的，我只是盡自己本分而已。我始終覺得，人的素質是最重要的，教育扶貧就是『授人以漁』。」

醫療扶貧：
消除六十萬人貧
困之源

疾病擋住了致富的腳步

健康和衛生在減少甚至消除貧困中的地位尤為重要。世界衛生組織總幹事陳馮富珍在二〇一五減貧與發展高層論壇上致辭時指出，衛生、健康與貧困至少在三方面都是緊密聯繫的。貧困會影響人們的健康，包括那些貧困的、不健康的、不衛生的環境，失業，缺乏營養以及使用藥物或者菸草，這些都對精神和身體的健康發起挑戰。更好的健康使得人們能夠更容易擺脫貧困。

在廣東一百七六點五萬相對貧困人口中，因病致貧比例達到百分之三十六點二。這意味著，疾病已成為橫亙在廣東超過六十萬人脫貧路上最大的「攔路虎」。病倒一個人就塌下一個家。如何讓農民病有所醫，是廣東扶貧中面臨的一大難題。

人均僅四分田地，養不活一家老小，這是粵東梅州溪口村的現實。人多地少，唯一的解決方案就是「走出大山，外出務工」。溪口人早就知道脫貧致富的出路。但並不是所有溪口人都能走出大山，去到縣城，再去到更遠的珠三角。當地很多家庭，其成員因病喪失了勞動能力，沒有富餘的勞力向山外輸出——病魔就如藤蔓，拴住了他們邁出大山、脫貧致富的腳步。

疾病面前，這些家庭餘下的一兩個勞動力，顯得形隻影單。溪口村地處廣東省梅州市大埔縣青溪鎮西部。二〇一〇年前，溪口村總人口一千七百四十八人，其中年收入一千五百元以下的貧困家庭一百八十一戶，貧困人口七百二十六人。全村水田二百四十二畝，人均僅四分田地，絕大部分人不得不外出務工。

在外闖蕩三十年後，劉長喜回到溪口，身無長物，三三二省道旁的一間土坯民房是他的全部。他努力了半生，試圖改變命運，但到最後，他還是敗給了疾病。

劉長喜是改革開放以後，當地最早外出務工的那批人之一。一九七七年，劉長喜離開溪口，因為只有小學文化，進不了國營廠礦，只能四處奔走，出賣勞力。劉長喜經人介紹，去了廣東省惠州市龍門縣，受僱於當地人，為其照看山上的經濟作物。十多年後，已經五十多歲的劉長喜才終於結婚，妻子小他十五歲，他的妻子有過一次婚姻經歷，是一名寡婦，還患有癲癇。

婚姻，讓劉長喜如浮萍般的命運有了歸屬，但也讓他漸有起色的生活重新晦暗。婚後，妻子常常犯病，為了給老婆治病，劉長喜四處尋醫問藥。二十世紀九〇年代初，「新農合」還沒有普及，老婆的醫療費、四處奔走的路費似沉重的負擔，令劉長喜窒息。

二〇一〇年，七十六歲的劉長喜一生與貧病糾纏，四十一歲的丁瑞輝步其後塵。二〇〇六年，丁瑞輝的妻子因病去世，為了照顧年邁的雙親和三個沒成年的女兒，老丁終止了打工生涯，回歸了農民身分。妻子去世前，丁家的生活有了起色，夫妻二人還回鄉蓋了兩間新磚房，但給妻子治病，老丁欠下了幾萬元的債務，四年後，錢還沒還清。

丁家目前六口人，只有三畝多田地。農忙後，老丁還要去茶陽鎮、青溪鎮做臨工。臨工收入不定，老丁手頭很少有餘錢，他一個勞力要供養六口人，給父母治病要花錢，大女兒讀中學需要生活費。

溪口村只是廣東貧困山區因為疾病而導致貧困的一部分人的縮

影。一部分外出人員的確脫貧了，但有些人因為沒文化，出去沒什麼好工作，賺錢也不易。扶貧幹部李慶祥認為，目前，大部分貧困山區的青壯年大部分都是初中畢業，完成了義務教育，就不讀書了，初中學歷，到外面也只能做最底層的活。

因病致貧，一方面是因為農民家庭經濟基礎薄弱，無力負擔醫療費用。另一方面則是因為疾病奪走了家庭成員的勞動能力，一個家庭只有壯年男性一個勞動力，導致家庭跌入貧困線。

李慶祥說，家庭成員因病喪失勞動力，甚至死亡，最後導致家境每況愈下，此類家庭占到貧困家庭裡的絕大多數。而一些家庭好不容易脫貧，卻又因病返貧，是困擾山區扶貧的難題。

所有的致貧原因最後串聯成一條線索：缺少田地，農民難以靠傳統農業致富，不得已，外出務工──囿於文化水平低，務工人員工資收入也低，家庭徘徊於窮苦之境──一些家庭為了治病導致經濟負擔增加，成員喪失勞動力（甚至死亡），這使得這些家庭成了最窮的那批人。

農村醫療的一波三折

在七年前，劉長喜所在的一個生產隊三百多人，只配有一間衛生院，衛生院的醫生還多是大專、中專學歷，要他們包治百病不可能，這是很多貧困山區醫療條件的現狀。

說是家醫院，卻治不了老百姓的病，衛生院的院長涂啟智談起七八年前的窘境也很無奈，他當時手下只有十名醫生、三名護士。

除了人少，衛生院的設施也很簡陋，當時最先進的設備也只是一台黑白 B 超。老醫生退休，衛生院一直找不到能頂上的醫生。涂啟智以前為此常常去大埔縣衛生局要人，可他也自知，招到醫生的可能性有限，「主要是衛生院小，工資低，沒有吸引力」。

作為院長，老涂當時每月的工資是一千五百多元，他手下的醫生，大專學歷的月工資七百多元，中專學歷的月工資六百多元。

由於鄉鎮衛生院的工資與城市醫院的工資差距大，有經驗的醫生大量外流，到衛生院看病的群眾也是逐年減少。

作為一名基層醫務人員，農民看病難，涂啟智感同身受。

目前，中國的基本醫保主要分為三種，分別是職工醫保、城鎮居民醫保、新農合。這其中，城鎮居民醫保由財政和城鎮居民繳費，由人社部門管理；新農合由財政和農民繳費，由衛計部門管理。

在二十世紀七〇年代，中國農村合作醫療制度與農村的縣、鄉、村 三級醫療保健制度、赤腳醫生一起成為解決我國廣大農村缺醫少藥 問題，保障人民群眾健康的農村醫療「三大法寶」，農村

合作醫療 模式被世界衛生組織和世界銀行盛讚為「以最少投入獲得最大健康 收益的模式」，並被作為樣板向第三世界國家推廣。一九七八年合作 醫療寫入《中華人民共和國憲法》，到農村生產責任制改革之前的一九七八年，全國農村合作醫療覆蓋率達到百分之八十到九十。

進入二十世紀八〇年代，全國農村實行家庭聯產承包責任制，人民公社被取消，生產大隊也隨之解體，農村集體經濟迅速萎縮，合作醫療制度快速走向解體，絕大部分村衛生室、合作醫療站變成了鄉村醫生的私人診所，農民缺醫少藥的現象再次出現。據調查，合作醫療覆蓋率由一九八〇年 68.8% 驟降到一九八三年的 20% 以下。據一九八五年的統計調查，全國實行合作醫療的行政村由過去的 90% 降到了 5%。在二十世紀九〇年代，我國政府推行「民辦公助，自願參加」的政策，兩度試圖重建農村合作醫療，但在制度設計上沒有明確社會保障國家主體責任的定位，恢復和建立的工作都沒有收到預期的成效。有一組數據可以說明當時農村合作醫療的窘境，國家財政衛生事業費用中用於農村合作醫療的補助費一九七九年是一億元，一九九二年下降到三千五百萬元，僅占衛生事業費用的百分之零點三六。

本世紀初，伴隨著城鄉發展不協調矛盾的日益突出，二〇〇二年十月中國重新開啟了農村合作醫療制度的建設工作，並把過去的農村合作醫療制度稱之為新型農村合作醫療制度。新農合除了針對日常門診和住院，大病保險也納入範疇。以廣州市為例，如今，農村居民只要繳納一百元／年的新農合費用，各級政府就會補貼三百四十元／年，農村居民就可以享受門診就醫百分之五十，住院治療百分之七十的報銷額度。如果發生重大疾病，在醫保報銷之後，個人自付部分還可以享受百分之五十以上的報銷。報銷最高限額為十五萬元一年。

　　二〇一六年年初，廣東實現了農村和城鎮人口兩種醫保制度相整合。廣東城鄉醫保並軌後，各地醫保定點的醫療機構、醫保藥品的目錄，都明顯擴大。尤其對不少新農合參保人來說，整合後醫保用藥範圍成倍增長。廣東城鄉醫保並軌後，城鄉居民統一使用基本醫保藥品目錄，農民的可報銷藥品種類分別從一千一百種、一千零八十三種、九百一十八種擴大到二千四百種、二千四百五十種、二千一百種，醫保用藥的範圍增加一倍多。

醫療扶貧：
「一條龍」健康扶貧到家

除了加強新農合醫保，廣東也在利用新制度和新技術來解決醫療扶貧問題。

連南地區是廣東省貧困落後地區，醫療衛生水平與全省平均水平有較大的差距。此前當地曾有三家大型醫院，但由於醫療技術與醫療環境水平有限，三家醫院都不能吸引病人，不少當地人會到鄰縣連州和連山看病，估計比例達到百分之四十以上。如何將紛紛趕赴外地治病的病人留在本地？

廣東藥學院相關負責人說，廣東藥學院幫扶性託管連南人民醫院，並不是出於商業目的，更多的是公益性、社會責任的擔當。而在託管之後，該院實行去行政化的法人代表管理模式，成立了負責醫院管理決策的董事會和監督董事會的監事會。醫院的所有職務都去行政化，取消行政級別，醫院的領導班子成員由董事會任命。廣東藥學院派出的管理團隊以及技術骨幹也極大提高了連南醫院的水平。

除了新農合制度和醫療下沉以外，新技術也為醫療扶貧難題提出解決方案。九十一歲高齡的梁保在六年前中風了，半身癱瘓的他活動範圍就是十幾平方米大小的屋子，就連想在家門口曬太陽都難，更不要說上醫院了。二〇一六年十月十六日，由廣東省第二人民醫院陽山醫院集團全體黨員及廣東省網絡醫院推出的陽山縣家庭醫生團隊，專程趕到梁保所在的清遠市陽山縣范村，與他簽約，並在未來提供免費的精準治療。這是省第二人民醫院陽山醫院集團對口幫扶推出的新福利。

廣東省扶貧辦二〇一六年八月公布的數據顯示，全省相對貧困戶主要致貧原因前三位分別是因病（36.2%）、缺勞力（23.3%）、因殘（19.9%）。清遠市陽山縣是貧困山區的一個縮影。陽山一共有一百五十九個村，廣東省網絡醫院院長周其如和下屬工作人員逐村篩查出了二千多戶「因病致貧、因病返貧」的貧困戶。

為了讓優質醫療資源下沉至基層，提升基層鄉村的醫療衛生服務能力，省第二人民醫院陽山醫院集團提出利用「互聯網+大眾醫療」技術來進行醫療扶貧。

專家們發現，在陽山，像梁保一樣不能出遠門看病的居民有很多，必須提供上門服務。廣東省網絡醫院線上線下的健康管理團隊，開始對他們進行「一條龍」的健康管理。

家庭醫生團隊由村醫、鎮衛生院公衛醫生、廣東省網絡醫院醫生、省第二人民醫院陽山醫院集團黨員及專家組成。簽約後，醫生將為簽約家庭建立完善居民健康檔案、更新健康檔案內容。此外，還將提供老、幼、婦和重大疾病、慢性疾病的追蹤服務和省、縣、鎮、村四級醫療機構的資源共享等個性化的優惠服務。

陽山這二千多戶「因病致貧、因病返貧」的貧困戶都將與家庭醫生團隊簽約。兩年內使這些貧困戶家中的患病人群全部得到免費的精準治療，同步對他們進行健康管理，從根本上改善他們的生活質量，使其脫貧致富。

如今劉長喜已經加入了新農合，隨著大病保險的覆蓋，他妻子的疾病報銷比例大幅提高，他的家庭困境得到了緩解。與此同時，隨著醫療力量的下沉，劉長喜所在的大隊迎來了兩名科班出身的社區醫生，劉長喜等不用再趕到十幾公里外的縣城看病問診了。

交通扶貧：
「修條好路給
農村既是出路
也是活路」

大動脈通了毛細血管卻沒通

改革開放將近四十年，在致富路上農民悟出了許多道理，其中最為顯著的是「要致富、先修路，富不富、先看路」，可見農村公路在我國經濟發展中的重要地位和作用。交通是制約經濟發展的瓶頸，而農村公路暢通與否又是農村經濟發展的關鍵。

廣東，作為中國改革開放春風最早吹過的省份，在交通運輸等基礎設施建設上一直領先於全國。到二○一五年年底，廣東高速公路通車里程達到七千零一十八公里，在全國率先突破七千公里，繼續保持領先水平。實現全省「縣縣通高速」目標，出省通道達到十七條，實現與陸路相鄰省份開通三條以上出省通道；粵東西北地區高速公路網絡也得到明顯改善，通車里程達到三千二百八十二公里，外通內連、協調均衡的高速公路骨幹網絡基本形成。一系列數字反映，廣東的道路設施投入並不少，成果也不小。可道路建設多集中在珠三角等經濟發達區域，對於粵東西北等山區，交通基礎設施的欠賬卻仍有不少。

廣東省河源市楊梅村曾經有很多大齡青年因交通閉塞娶不到媳婦，「小夥子長得都很好，有什麼辦法呢？」對於貧窮的肇因，村民們無不指出，「路太爛」。

出村難，成為楊梅人最深刻的記憶。早些年，楊梅人到河源市區辦事。早上七時三十分出發，走山路二小時到錫場鎮碼頭，再坐船擺渡，中午十二時三十分才能抵達河源，下午萬一沒辦成事，只能花錢住旅館。

村民天天都盼著修好路

村民詹石源，曾在二○○一年種過幾十畝果樹。「因為這條破山路，老闆不願來收，來了還不斷壓價，外面賣一元，這裡只賣三五毛。」因交通不便，幾乎所有村民每次種養都虧本。不管青菜還是水果，外面收貨的車都要在東面七公里的山外等。楊梅村有一台部隊退役下來的爛炮車，「只有它能把貨從爛泥路中運出去」。加上人工過車費、僱車費及等待的費用，村民們運貨每車的成本為一百五十到二百元。

二○○八年，錫場鎮禾石坑村一個農民在庫區成功培育靈芝，收入可觀，隨後靈芝被推廣至全鎮，東源縣甚至將錫場鎮定為「靈芝專業鎮」。靈芝培育，一夜間似乎成了楊梅村脫貧的靈丹妙藥。「第一年種的人賺了幾千元，第二年村民們一擁而上，十多戶培育面積達十二畝。」二○○九年村民李業生用東風卡車運了六大車木頭，光種子就花了六千元，培育了二千五百多斤靈芝。

可刺痛楊梅人是，到了五月份木樁裡種子全部發黑，一堆堆蒸好、培上種子的木頭只能用來燒火。「到現在還搞不清原因，很多人說是感染了，但沒有專家願意進山指導我們。」

二○○七年經過爭取，村東側十點五公里鎮通村公路被修通。但西側七公里的經濟路，村民爭取了多次始終沒有立項。國家扶貧開發領導小組的調研人員，對東部省份的扶貧開發工做作了調查，調研人員發現，廣東貧困地區基礎設施欠賬較大，與產業發展需要非常不適應，改善貧困人口的生產生活條件仍然是一項繁重的任務。

　　直到二〇一二年，幫扶單位才在楊梅村實現了村西側七公里經濟路項目的立項審批，籌資二百四十餘萬元，準備讓這條經濟路在當年年底修通。

修條好路既是出路也是活路

　　泗水村是上一輪（2013-2015 年）「雙到」扶貧中的被幫扶村莊，已順利脫貧。省人大代表、梅州市平遠縣泗水鎮泗水村黨支部書記、村委會主任王滿秀介紹，從上一輪「雙到」扶貧得出的經驗是，貧困村民要想脫貧致富，必須先把村裡的道路修好。泗水村村民主要是種蔬菜、種樹。沒有路，客商進不來，東西運不出去，只能爛在地裡。泗水村的情況在貧困村中普遍存在，道路等基礎設施不完善，是造成貧困的一個重要因素。不少貧困村與泗水村類似，並不是缺乏資源或產業，只是受限於交通閉塞、道路不暢等原因，優質的農產品難以對外銷售，良好的旅遊資源無法得到開發和推介。農民不出去、企業進不來，天然有機的農產品爛在了地裡，秀麗宜人的自然風光掩埋在了深山，農民坐擁豐富的自然資源，卻無法進行開發利用，日子越過越貧困。

　　加快農村經濟發展，必須加大農村公路建設，加強農村公路管理，改善交通運輸環境，為農村產業結構調整和商品流通鋪平道路，促進農民增收致富。

　　廣東要在二〇一八年率先全面建成小康社會，脫貧攻堅是必須取勝的關鍵戰役。抓好農村基礎設施建設作為精準扶貧精準脫貧的八項工程之一，不僅要把路修通，而且要構建互相串聯、有效貫通的交通體系，從而發展產業、盤活資源、增加收入，增強貧困村的「造血功能」。

　　廣東省交通廳制訂計畫，到二〇一八年，在縣縣通高速公路基礎上，進一步完善貧困地區高速公路網絡。以縣鄉公路路面改造為重點，加強貧困地區縣鄉道建設。

全國人大代表，清遠連南瑤族自治縣寨崗鎮山聯村黨支部書記、村委會主任何桂芳所在的村曾因交通滯後，信息閉塞，發展落後，被當地人稱為連南的「西伯利亞」。多年來，在何桂芳的多方呼籲下，村裡的路通了，電通了，發展加快，村民生活逐漸改善。他認為，廣東集中力量改善貧困地區的生產生活條件，就是要補齊農村發展短板。「要修條好路給農村。對農民來講，這是出路，也是活路。」全國人大代表、廣東中山紀念中學原校長賀優琳說。

金融扶貧：
加速脫貧之路

農業「缺錢」之痛：
春耕資金缺口大

說起廣東的貧困地區，很多人都以為在粵東西北地區，其實在珠三角地區也有貧困存在。金坑村位於「江門五邑」之一的恩平東成鎮，面積十點四平方公里，包括五個自然村，四百七十一戶，總人口一千四百九十九人。耕地二千三百畝，主要以附加值低的水稻種植為主，村人均年收入三千一百元左右。村民除出國做生意外，也有部分到恩平、江門、中山、廣州等地打工。

資金是制約金坑村農業發展的主要問題之一。

一九九五年，恩平爆發因高息攬儲帶來的銀行擠兌危機，銀行接連倒閉，十餘年時間內當地金融機構的發展一度非常蕭條。當地商業銀行大幅收縮服務網點，由發生風險前的二百六十六個減少到現在的四十三個。

而在農村地區，由於恩平城鄉信用社已經撤銷，金融服務只能依靠郵政儲蓄銀行得以維繫，其他金融機構要麼沒有農業金融服務，要麼「只存不貸」。相關數據顯示，截至二〇〇七年底當地所有的農業貸款餘額僅有四十八萬元，僅占江門地區農業貸款總額的百分之〇點〇三。

金坑村只是廣東廣大貧困農村的一個縮影。一九九八年以來，金融對「三農」的支持基本空白。最基本的水稻種植方面，也缺乏資金支持。據恩平市農業局測算，二〇〇六年恩平全市春耕資金需求約五千零四十萬元，農民自有資金約一千一百八十萬元，資金缺口高達三千八百六十萬元。

農業保險缺位：
金融風險農民獨擔

「恩平地處珠三角，交通便利，市場大，種養業按說很有市場。」恩平市農業局副局長馮浪其說，養殖等不但需要技術、資金，農業保險也要跟上。

但農業保險遲遲不能跟上。據瞭解，從二○○六年開始，恩平市保險業界對效益相對低下的農業項目涉入較少，嘗試性開辦的個別農業險種（水果種植），由於長期虧損，目前已基本停止辦理。農業保險缺失，不能有效分散農業風險，而相應的風險補償機制又未建立，進一步制約著金融機構對農村建設的投入，形成惡性循環。

二○○六年，鄉村銀行的創辦者，被譽為「窮人的銀行家」的尤努斯教授憑此獲得諾貝爾和平獎。消息使中國備受鼓舞，開放農村金融市場的改革新政由此醞釀。

二○○六年十二月，銀監會出台政策首次允許產業資本和民間資本到農村地區新設銀行，並提出要在農村增設村鎮銀行、貸款公司和農村資金互助社等三類金融機構，被金融業界稱作第四輪中國農村金融改革破冰之舉。

「小額貸款難，這在全國農村來說具有一定的普遍性。」中國社會科學院農村發展研究所研究員張元紅表示，盈利作為銀行主要的營業目標，不斷加強成本結算，在收縮過於分散的農村網點的同時將貸款額度的審批權開始上收，目前縣以下的營業網點基本上沒有審批貸款的權力。

讓金融重返農村

事實上，金融服務力度在農村的的不足已引起各方的重視。

二〇〇九年，廣東有六十多個零銀行業金融機構網點的鄉鎮，主要分布在粵東、粵西和粵北經濟不發達、金融業規模比較小的區域。二〇一〇至二〇一三年，廣東通過逐步推進新型農村金融機構試點類型和范圍、鼓勵商業銀行和農村信用社增設機構網點等方式，才逐步填補了零銀行業金融機構網點鄉鎮的空白。

村鎮銀行的模式也被引入中國，在小範圍內進行試點。二〇〇七年底，廣東正式開始籌劃新型農村金融機構試點工作。恩平和乳源被選定為廣東的首批試點地區。二〇〇九年三月，匯豐恩平村鎮銀行正式開業，引入「公司+農戶」的小額信貸業務：圍繞當地較大的農業龍頭企業，向與其長年發生業務往來的農戶和經銷商提供相應的貸款，重點支持恩平農村居民、城鎮居民、農村小微企業和農業中小企業金融的需求。

為發展「三農」，中國目前正推出系列政策：鼓勵大型商業股份制銀行下鄉，主動向農民提供小額貸款，幫助發展生產；在條件成熟的發達地區，增加營業網點，方便農民辦理貸款業務；進行新型農村金融體制的創新，成立農村戶主組織和小額貸款公司，幫助農民解決貸款難的問題。

一些貧困地區缺乏有效的經濟增長模式和商業模式，金融資本難以有效進入，難以形成可持續性。面對擔保難、抵押物不足、貸款主體不合格等困擾貧困地區脫貧的「老大難」問題，廣東銀行業圍繞農村綜合改革，創新配套金融產品，結合農民「融資難」、農村「金融貧血」等「癥結」開出多元化「藥方」。

為了破解擔保難的問題，廣東清遠銀行業針對八百餘戶已確權的土地承包經營權，創新推出了「流轉貸」產品。「在農村土地確權登記頒證的基礎上，農民可以根據自身需要，向農業銀行申請貸款，把土地資源轉化為貸款資金。」中國農業銀行廣東清遠分行副行長李亮表示。

廣東英德市農村信用合作社瞭解當地情況之後，創新推出「農改貸」產品，適度放寬了對借款主體必須經工商部門註冊登記的限制，向耕地分散的英德市石牯塘鎮螢火村葉屋村經濟合作社授信二百萬元，支持其開展土地流轉，提高土地利用效率。

為實現精準扶貧，廣東省委推行「駐村幫扶+建檔立卡」模式，在全省範圍內積極開展扶貧「雙到」工作，即「規劃到戶、責任到人」，駐村幫扶，定村定戶，定責定人，一定三年，限期脫貧。

該模式為建檔立卡貧困戶提供專門的扶貧小額信貸，確保資金投放到生產，投放到就業。廣東銀監局鼓勵銀行業金融機構在准確評定貧困戶信用等級和還款能力的基礎上，向有貸款意願、有就業創業潛質、有技能素質的建檔立卡貧困戶提供五萬元以下、三年以內的信用貸款，滿足其生產、創業、就業、搬遷安置等各類貸款需求，同時對扶貧小額信貸實行利率優惠。

技術反哺
扶貧路

貧困戶手機淘寶賣聖女果

二〇一六年春節前，「超級寒潮」南下，廣東大部分地區遭到冰雪襲擊，長年「看天吃飯」的農產品大量減產。然而，在湛江、清遠連州等地，部分貧困村農民卻並未因為減產而收入大減，有些甚至獲得了比往年更好的收入。帶來這種變化的是如今為廣東各地扶貧幹部們所津津樂道、廣泛傳播的「電商扶貧」「移動互聯網扶貧」。

春節剛過，塘頭村的貧困村民羅儒廷已經接到了幾箱聖女果的訂單，正準備到田間收果發貨。因為節前的寒潮，田間的聖女果種苗有些已經乾枯。「今年掛果不多，早上摘，下午就發貨，用班車送到廣州。」羅儒廷隨手在田間摘下幾把微微泛紅的聖女果，「這種七八成熟的就可以摘了，這樣待果子在路上自然熟透，送到買家手中剛剛好」。

羅儒廷種的聖女果品種叫做「千禧」。「千禧」品種是二〇一四年由廣州駐湛江扶貧幹部通過電商平台上獲取的信息，從海南引進。正是「千禧」的引進，改變了塘頭村的聖女果廣種薄收又沒有好價錢的窘境。

二〇一三年之前，羅儒廷種的幾畝「萬福」聖女果，由於被批發商收購壓價，收成僅能勉強維持妻子的藥錢和孩子的學費。村黨支部委員、村民羅祝說：「以前聖女果的收購價一斤大概只有五毛錢，現在千禧的收購價至少都要一塊起，除去種子、肥料、人工費，每畝果子的利潤能有一點五萬元。」

曾經對智能手機一竅不通的羅儒廷，如今已經熟悉了電商的運作，負責接塘頭村的訂單，並組織貨源發貨。他打開手機展示「湛江駐村人扶貧專營店」的微店頁面，上面的農產品琳瑯滿目。

　　「田裡信號不好，我們通常都去村委會的電腦上查看訂單。」羅儒廷稱，村委會現在只有一台電腦，正準備用市裡的財政專項撥款採購幾台新的電腦。

　　他還頗為自豪地說：「我們的聖女果在上面是賣得最好的，還有北京、天津、上海的訂單。」如今，塘頭村聖女果的訂單來源已經覆蓋整個珠三角。接到訂單後，羅儒廷就會組織收購，用快遞或班車發出去。僅二〇一五年十二月，他就接到了十幾筆大訂單，跟了四趟車送貨到廣州。

　　岑宇鏗是廣州駐湛江雷州塘頭村的扶貧幹部，「農產品電商」的發起人。在塘頭村民眼中，「這個個子不高、年紀不大、戴著眼鏡、斯斯文文的廣州小夥子，很能幹」！在岑宇鏗看來，塘頭村的土地以沙地為主，比較貧瘠，地少人多，農業排灌設施差。三百零三戶村民中，就有一百零五戶貧困戶，脫貧任務非常重。

　　「我們到村裡後，發現最大的問題，就是農民無法瞭解市場的信息，一直都是靠原有的種植技術去種植農產品，包括聖女果。」岑宇鏗說，此前聖女果苗和種子都是收購商提供的，收購商不僅壓價嚴重，「還會扣除百分之十的爛果率的錢」。「即使農民有一定的利潤空間，但不足以讓他們脫貧致富。」

　　他想到了已經在全國大城市中發展得轟轟烈烈的移動互聯網。二〇一四年三月二十五日，淘寶上的「塘頭村扶貧農產品專營店」正式上線，塘頭村成為最早「試水」電商扶貧的地方。

據中國工信部通報，二〇一六年中國移動電話用戶規模達到十二點八億，移動互聯網用戶總數達九點八億戶。如今移動互聯網已深刻影響人們的生活。

　　在美國上市的阿里巴巴公司所擁有的淘寶網是中國深受歡迎的網購零售平台，目前擁有近五億的註冊用戶，每天有超過六千萬的固定訪客，同時每天的在線商品數已經超過了八億件，平均每分鐘售出四點八萬件商品。而騰訊公司所屬的微信日活躍用戶量超過了六點七億人次。目前，在中國大中型城市，人們出門可以不用攜帶現金和信用卡，餐飲、服裝、超市等消費場所幾乎都與互聯網支付接軌。甚至連醫院、出租車、停車場和高速公路都能用手機完成付費。

　　「村裡的農民和貧困戶開始不理解，他們認為電商很虛，不能夠真的幫到他們。」為了讓村民信任「電商」，岑宇鏗找到了當地最大的收購商，並與其合作，先在淘寶店上幫貧困戶賣聖女果。結果，僅二〇一四年上半年，就幫助農戶銷售「萬福」聖女果達三萬多斤。與此同時，岑宇鏗等人在電商平台上瞭解到，海南有一種叫「千禧」的聖女果，國內少有地方種植，價值更高。於是，駐村幹部從海南買來了嫁接苗，開出了一百畝的「千禧」基地，並邀請海南的專家對在基地裡務工的貧困戶進行技術培訓。

　　二〇一五年元旦後，「千禧」聖女果大量上市，並在淘寶店上熱賣，吸引了大量買家。二〇一五年「千禧」基地營收超過兩百萬元，單是支付給貧困戶農民採摘、包裝等勞務工資就超過七十萬元。二〇一六年一月份，基地聖女果上市，田頭收購價達到了每市斤七點五元。二〇一五年十月起，塘頭村「千禧」種植面積已經從一百畝，變成了三百五十畝，幾乎所有村民都種起了「千禧」品種。

早在二〇一四年十月，塘頭村的農產品電商經驗被廣州駐湛江扶貧工作隊推廣到了整個湛江的九十五個貧困村，淘寶店的名字也改成了「湛江駐村人扶貧專營店」。在「湛江駐村人扶貧專營店」上，九十五個村的農產品均可在上面展示、銷售，聖女果、香瓜、黑米、紅米、黑山羊、火龍果以及海產品等應有盡有。

如今，整個雷州半島的農民都跟著種起了「千禧」聖女果，面積超過三千畝。通過電商扶貧，扶貧幹部還與村民們一起建立了青棗、香瓜、火龍果基地，種植面積超過六千畝。除此之外，他們還引入了黑米、紅米、東方一號密瓜等優質農產品，生產廣受追捧的芝麻花生油。

截至二〇一六年二月底，通過電商平台對接珠三角、長三角和京津冀等市場，湛江地區貧困戶各類農產品線上線下銷售額早已突破千萬元。廣州駐湛扶貧工作隊還建立起了「電商平台+種植倉儲加工產業基地+合作社+農戶」的模式。這為當地貧困村建立穩定脫貧長效機制提供了很好的平台，據統計，電商扶貧惠及湛江地區貧困戶達三萬戶。

如今，羅儒廷、羅祝等塘頭村的村民已經熟悉了網上銷售農產品的流程，而三年來的「電商扶貧」，已經在湛江九十五個貧困村產生了巨大的「電商效應」。駐村幹部們還幫助村民們成立了一個由十二戶農戶組成的農民專業合作社，已經能夠帶動八十八戶貧困戶，並以此帶動其他八十八戶貧困戶脫貧。

二〇一五年五月至八月，岑宇鏗受國務院全國貧困地區幹部深圳培訓基地邀請，先後為西藏、雲南、江西、河南、湖南、湖北及廣東七個 省、自治區的扶貧幹部講授電商扶貧。在岑宇鏗看來，電商扶貧實際上只是「互聯網+農業」的一個探索，由國家層面推進才可以真正解決貧困地區農產品的銷售。

他認為，官方應儘快建立農業大數據庫，不僅對農業企業開放，更要對普通農民開放。「比如氣候的大數據、農產品價格的大數據、地域性的產品的對比、種子商出售種子的數據等等，大的電商平台都可以開放自己的數據庫給農民。如果實在不行，那就由政府來購買這些數據，並對農民開放。」

「村長大米」入住蘇寧易購

台山沖蔞鎮的前鋒村是一條貧困村，村民基本以農耕為主。村民耕種出來的稻穀如何賣得好，一直是一個「老大難」問題。由於受海水倒灌、鹽鹼地較多的影響，村集體收入一直沒有起色。三年前，江門市扶貧開發「雙到」工作組駐村扶貧後，想方設法為村民解決農產品銷路問題。

台山沖蔞鎮前鋒村扶貧工作組組長譚俊彥發現，不少村民並沒有發揮主觀能動性。為此扶貧工作組請來了一位「八〇後」村長廖傑良。「八〇後」村長廖傑良早年外出打工，一直想用在外打工的經驗把家鄉建設好。他發現，前鋒村一千八百人一共有一千七百畝水稻，人均水稻不足一畝，除此之外，村裡還有一千三百畝香蕉林，二百八十畝森林。而村子裡除了老人和小孩外，百分之六十的年輕人都出門務工。廖傑良說，「農產品是貧困戶主要的收入來源，解決到它的銷路的話，基本上就可以解決（貧困戶）的大部分收入了。」

通過政府牽線搭橋，蘇寧易購中華特色館台山館的運營團隊來到了前鋒村，將該村的一千七百百畝水稻全部打包收購，解決了村民們賣糧難的後顧之憂。蘇寧易購中華特色館台山館運營負責人何恆慶說：「江門二〇一五年也發生過這個馬鈴薯滯銷的問題，啟發了我們啟動中華特色館台山館農產品的銷售的初衷，加上台山扶貧的宗旨和目的，希望蘇寧易購台山館能解決台山貧困村農產品滯銷的問題。」

除了線上蘇寧台山館，台山市還在線上推出了「扶貧 APP」。「扶貧 APP」最大限度集納了貧困村、貧困戶的信息以及針對他們開展精準扶貧的多種活動和形式，突破了傳統幫扶模式，今後一系列線上線下的低成本幫扶活動均可通過此渠道漸次展開。

　　該款 APP 軟件近期首個幫扶活動是「愛心菜籃」，置於「公益眾籌」模塊中。其形式是以當前台山市九百二十戶貧困戶所種植的優質農產品為扶貧產品，推出「愛心九九幸福菜籃」（取「愛心久久」之義）一千份，每份九十九元，所得收益全部給貧困戶，以解決他們的銷售困境。

網上求職「通道」
鋪到家門口

　　「動動筆，填張報名表，在家裡就能等到就業的機會，省去了很多麻煩。」近日，河頭鎮灣中村貧困戶練成健家裡收到了這樣的「工作報名表」。新興縣推進精準扶貧精準脫貧、引入人力資源實時招聘平台——淘力網絡科技有限公司（以下簡稱「淘力」），並根據貧困戶實際情況，「量身定制」了「網上求職申請表格」。

　　根據駐村扶貧幹部的指引，練成健完善了個人信息、工作經驗及就業意向等簡歷情況。練成健說，駐村扶貧幹部會幫助他把簡歷上傳至淘力平台進行職位匹配，平台也將通過手機客戶端把工作信息推送到他手中，「一旦匹配成功，就能參加應聘了」。

　　練成健二十二歲，剛剛大專畢業，「求職難」是他畢業以來最大的感受。相比之下，由駐村幹部協助錄入個人信息，通過淘力平台實時求職，等待匹配職位和應聘，比起在各招聘網站盲目地投簡歷，要省去各種不必要的麻煩，也更容易獲得就業機會。

　　對此，練成健舉了一個例子：畢業之後，他為了找工作，曾通過各種招聘網站、手機軟件投遞簡歷達一百多份，但由於學歷不高，缺乏相應的工作經驗，求職之路屢屢碰壁。如今，他在廣州某公司工作，實習期工資二千三百元，扣除日常生活所需的花銷，所剩無幾。

　　練成健說，他希望能通過淘力平台獲得一份更好的工作，對於工資福利薪酬，期望能達到三千元或以上。「如果月薪能達到三千元或以上，我就能節省更多的錢寄回家裡，讓家裡儘快擺脫貧困狀態。」

經過全面核查，截至六月底，新興縣共核准相對貧困戶七千零五十四戶一萬六千六百八十一人，而要實現全面脫貧，首要解決的就是二千四百四十六戶九千五百六十九人有勞動能力的貧困戶的就業問題，幫助貧困戶通過就業實現脫貧。

然而，受制於地理位置、交通不便、信息滯後等因素，貧困戶找工作，大都只能依靠親戚朋友介紹，到城市找工作往往費時費力不討好。幫助貧困戶就業，成為三年精準扶貧的重點和難點。新興縣引入的淘力平台採取「互聯網+勞動力就業」的模式，面向全部建 檔立卡貧困戶勞動力，以淘力平台互聯網 O2O 模式運作，通過手機客戶端將工作崗位信息推送到貧困戶手中。同時，貧困戶還可通過淘力職業技術培訓提高技能，找到更好的工作，獲得更高的收入。

新興縣扶貧辦工作人員張志軍介紹，為了創造更多的就業機會，新興縣與淘力就業平台簽訂了合作協議，淘力也為此專門成立新興縣精準扶貧項目組，雙方就如何為貧困戶提供就業崗位的推介和職業培訓的項目進行了多次研究。

考慮到個別貧困戶沒有智能手機，淘力專門為其設置和印製紙質工作報名表，這樣，貧困戶通過報名表，由駐村幹部協助貧困戶通過手機客戶端「淘力實時招聘平台」實時求職，也可以由貧困戶自行通過手機客戶端錄入個人信息資料即時求職。

日前，新興縣扶貧辦組織十五個重點村的駐村幹部、第一書記等召開新興縣精準脫貧「勞動力就業扶貧工程」培訓暨工作推進會。年內，淘力公司將為貧困戶提供多個工作崗位，如面向十八到五十歲女性提供家政服務崗位，面向十八到五十歲貧困戶提供技工、普工、倉庫管理、品質檢驗、銲接工、電工等工作崗位。

高鐵改變了
的大山生活

高鐵帶來人氣、財氣

　　初夏的貴州，清風和煦，陽光燦爛，一片片翠綠的茶園裡，茶農像往年一樣在茶園裡忙碌著。而在貴廣高鐵另一頭的廣東，一台台電腦正在飛速上網，聯繫著茶葉的銷路。這樣的改變與往年不同，科技信息與交通設施越發發達，貴州的茶農茶商和廣東的茶葉批發商們，正乘著互聯網大數據這朵「雲」，不斷提升貴州茶葉質量安全公信度，用互聯網做大茶產業；同時，藉著貴廣高鐵開通、融入珠三角三小時經濟圈的「東風」，茶山扶貧經濟正在崛起。

　　鐵路作為國民經濟大動脈、國家重要基礎設施和大眾化交通工具，多年來，鐵路部門在確保人們安全便捷出行的同時，也在沿途的貧困地區扶貧開發和區域經濟協調發展上發揮了重要作用。「鐵路一通，黃金萬兩」，中國的這一說法就是表明鐵路作為打通各地經濟命脈的連接線的重要性。

　　一九九八年，廣梅汕鐵路（連接廣州、梅州和汕頭）開通初期，沿線龍川、五華、興寧、豐順等縣均是「國家級貧困縣」，到二〇一六年，這幾縣全部走出了「國家級貧困縣」序列。隨著廣州至梅州至汕頭鐵路提速擴能、惠梅汕高鐵建設逐步鋪開，沿線地區將再次迎來發展良機。

　　與此同時，二〇〇九年開通的武廣高鐵（武漢至廣州）途經區域已經「隆起」了一條「大產業帶」。武廣高鐵二〇〇九年開通迄今六年，沿 途的韶關、清遠以及湘鄂高鐵沿線城市共承接珠三角產業轉移項目一萬多個，總投資突破五千億元。二〇一五年，清

遠、韶關等高鐵沿線 城市的 GDP 增長率均在 8%以上，增幅高出
全省其他各市，均較無高鐵 前的二〇〇八年高了五個百分點。

▌列車上曾經的「動物園」

　　歷時十八個多小時，經過八百五十七千米，這是以往從貴州開往廣東的列車專線的時間和距離。從上個世紀開始，貴州和廣東的「慢列車」已經運行了近半個世紀。常年穿梭於這個列車上的劉文成回憶道，通常在火車的最後一節車廂——行李車廂，許多乘客會圍在一起。旁邊堆放著幾個裝滿活雞的大背簍。對於六十一歲的劉文成來說，這條線他再熟悉不過了。

　　二十年前，他就是坐這趟車把貴州山上收集的茶葉帶到廣東售賣。二十年後，他依舊在靠著這條鐵路增收致富。每隔半個月，這位老人便會和三五夥伴一起，背著收好的茶葉，步行一個多小時，趕在十三時零一分之前登上駛往廣東的火車。每斤二十元收，三十元賣。除去車費，劉文成一次可以賺上五百多元。

　　每年賣茶葉的幾千元收入，已經成為他家庭收入的重要補充。「火車方便、票價低，我們才能賺到錢。」劉文成講述時，對鐵路給他帶來的便利心滿意足。

　　在二十多年前，除了茶葉，車廂遠處，成群的鴨鵝，叫聲此起彼伏，幾隻山羊在車廂裡互相爭鬥，儼然一派「動物園」的場景。說話間，一隻鵝下了個蛋，引得滿堂哄笑。早在二十多年前，為了方便沿線貴州少數民族村民攜帶牲口趕集貿易，貴州部分列車專門打造了「行李車廂」安置牲口和大件行李，沿途車站還配備了專供牲口上下車使用的梯子。穿行在這兒的扶貧「慢列車」，已經成為拉動沿線經濟發展和百姓生活的重要「引擎」。

如今，「慢列車」消失了，「行李車廂」的使命也早已告一段落，現在連接貴州和廣東的是一條時速高達三百五十公里的高速鐵路，貴州和廣州的兩省生活從二十一個小時變成了五個半小時。

從「頓頓紅苕包穀飯，吃水要翻幾匹山」到「吃水不用抬，做飯不燒柴」，四十多年「低頭種茶」讓貴州省湄潭縣核桃壩村逐漸脫離了貧困。隨著貴廣高鐵的開通，從「修大壩、種茶園、戶戶通馬路」到「創品牌、搞聯合、互聯網營銷」，短短數年間，原本只會「抬頭看天」的茶農，現在已經把眼光瞄向更廣的市場。

從種茶到收購茶青、加工製茶，從事茶產業十多年的湄潭縣湄江鎮核桃壩村茶農景林波除了擁有自己的茶葉公司外，還建起了占地近六畝的製茶作坊。

但靠零售和批發為主的茶生意並不能讓這位三十來歲的年輕人滿意。每斤茶葉去掉成本，也就賺十幾、二十元錢加工費，還經常被壓價，沒啥利潤空間，景林波認為，需要從低端往上走，景林波將目光放在了塑造品牌上。景林波決心打造自己的品牌。隨著貴廣高鐵的開通，交通運輸成本大大降低，隨著人流、物流的你來我往，茶農們終於掙脫了交通不便帶來的困境，核桃壩村也開始走出貧困。

湄潭縣是貴州主要茶產區，種植面積五十多萬畝，二〇一四年茶葉綜 合收入超過三十億元。作為湄潭縣茶產業、茶文化的源頭，核桃壩村更是「因茶而興」。全村一萬多畝茶園，八百六十八戶村民家家戶戶種茶或加工茶，早就名揚茶界的核桃壩茶葉更是被廣東的茶商大量收購。

二〇一四年，當地農民人均純收入達到了一點四二萬元，但越來越多的茶農不再滿足於做產業鏈條中利潤最少的一環，互聯網成了茶農開拓市場的「利器」。從二〇一四年年底開始，茶農劉聲彥就一直忙著開發微信訂閱號、服務號，傳送「芸香茶葉」相關資訊，通過美文美圖傳播，讓更多的人知曉湄潭綠茶。目前，核桃壩村已有幾十家企業在天貓、京東等大型電商網站上建立了自己的網絡銷售渠道，銷售額逐年提高。

如何把種茶變成產業，讓自己從茶農蛻變為茶商？茶農劉澤遠打算聯合村裡的茶葉加工大戶，成立一家茶葉「聚集公司」，聯手實現不壓價、不賒賬，以解決投資成本少、資金回籠慢等經營難題。如今，縣裡每年都會帶領大批茶農、生產企業參加國內的各類農產品交易會、茶葉博覽會等以便尋找商機。

高鐵精準扶貧為
特殊旅客免費

二〇一七年一月十八日，廣州南至百色 D3782、廣州南至貴陽北 D2812、深圳北至武漢 G1010、深圳西至吉首 K9064 等四趟「幸福列車」滿載著三千多名旅客，先後從廣州和深圳發出，奔赴桂黔鄂湘四省份。這些旅客身分有些特殊，他們分別是創客一族、往年的「摩託大軍」以及精準扶貧對象。

周剛毅是「指舞互動」VR 遊戲開發團隊合夥人之一。他們共同開發了炫酷的 VR 產品，如「神遊敦煌莫高窟」等。在高鐵上，周剛毅的演示引起了很多人的關注。他說：「每個年輕人都有創業的夢想，現在國家政策這麼好，只要踏實去做，就一定有成功的可能。」

湖南省吉首市、廣西壯族自治區百色市、貴州省貴陽市均為廣東省的對口扶貧地區。從深圳到吉首的 K9064 次普鐵也是參與扶貧的專列。春運前夕，廣鐵集團聯合媒體發布招募信息，重點招募湖南吉首、花垣縣十八洞村及其周邊在廣東務工的建檔立卡扶貧對象、技工院校貧困學生、在粵貧困務工青年，由廣東省人社廳和愛心企業贈送返鄉專列火車票。廣鐵安排吉首籍鐵路列車員擔當值乘服務任務，並在列車上舉行愛心活動。

擔當列車服務工作的鐵路職工梁永寧是殘障人士，也是「寶貝回家」公益組織發起人之一，曾獲評「微博二〇一六十大影響力公益大 V」。他以個人名義捐助十張火車票幫助十八洞村建檔立卡扶貧對象回家過年。獲得免費車票之一的段光明是一名退伍軍人，經對口幫扶在深圳一家電子廠上班，一個月收入能有五千元左右，家裡情況逐步改善。

　　廣州南至貴州、百色的兩趟高鐵扶貧專列上，服務群體不僅有在廣東務工的建檔立卡扶貧對象，還有每年需要扶助關愛的「摩託大軍」。由於廣東和廣西、貴州各地摩托車限行越來越普遍，貴廣南廣高鐵運力二○一六年春運提升了百分之二十，每天可以運輸七萬名旅客，因此在延續二○一五年春運開行摩託大軍返鄉專列的基礎上，二○一六年繼續開行愛心高鐵專列，讓更多「摩託大軍」回家之路更為安全、舒適。

特色小鎮：
其實大山裡
也很好

_____

廣州「北大荒」變身

　　呂田鎮蓮麻村位於廣州市最北部，這裡北鄰韶關市新豐縣，東臨惠州市龍門縣，被譽為廣州的「北大門」。近年來，空氣清新、寧靜優美的自然環境讓蓮麻村的旅遊資源被「盯」上，大力發展蓮麻村被納入從化區「美麗小鎮」建設項目之一，蓮麻村已經搖身一變，讓許多人不再認識當年的貧困村。隨著「美麗小鎮」的變化，大山裡的日子越來越好，在不久的將來，大山的日子反而成為城市人們嚮往的生活。

　　蓮麻村共有十一個經濟社，人口一千四百零六人，是廣州市面積最大的一條行政村。蓮麻村以山地為主，由於受到地形因素限制，這裡不適宜種植一般的蔬菜，農作物以三華李、沙糖橘為主。「過去，村民收入主要來源於經濟林，後來由於國家出台大力保護森林資源的政策，村經濟收入以林業為主的傳統模式被打破。村民只能靠水源保護林的保護經費作為收入，並且很多有勞動能力的村民都選擇外出務工。」蓮麻村黨支部書記潘光灶說。由於該村地處偏遠，農民經濟來源少，過去曾經被從化當地人稱為嫁女都嫌棄的「北大荒」。

　　呂田鎮最北部的蓮麻村的貧困狀況縈繞在鎮、村幹部心頭，如何有效整合利用現有資源，走出一條屬於自己村的發展之路，在他們的心中打上了問號。二〇一四年底，廣州市領導到蓮麻村調研，給蓮麻村指出發展生態旅遊的方向，帶來了新的機遇。二〇一五年，從化區決定把蓮麻村打造成「美麗小鎮」，這個契機如同春風一般給蓮麻村帶來了改革的溫度，使之在一年多的時間裡遍地開滿了改革之花。從二〇一三年七月開始，廣州開展了對蓮麻村進行了三年多的幫扶，使該村面貌煥然一新。二〇一六年，經過精準幫扶後的蓮麻村集體收入達到五十六點五三萬元，村中二十戶貧困戶家庭人均年收入達到一點五萬元以上，搖身一變成為被周圍村鎮羨慕的「北大倉」。

「美麗小鎮」的建設給蓮麻村帶來了翻天覆地的改變，村民紛紛表示，他們能感受到最直觀的變化是村容村貌改善了，村民收入增加了。

基礎設施建設乃是最大的民生工程，蓮麻村的改造提升亦是從最基本的惠民設施建設開始。潘光灶介紹，近一年來，蓮麻村逐漸形成了美麗鄉村建設規模，基礎設施建設發生了很大變化，包括道路、河堤、綠道、停車場、污水設施等都在如火如荼建設當中，目前已完成了四公里的河堤建設和十二公里的綠道建設，而從G105 線到蓮麻村黃沙坑經濟社共三點一公里長的社道已改造成瀝青路。在環境方面，村委附近一帶增加了不少園林綠化景觀，帶來了耳目一新的景象。

▌農民變身民宿「掌櫃」

　　現在，從廣州經高速可直達蓮麻村附近，高速公路的陸續貫通為這座北部山區農村帶來人氣及商業機會。二〇一六年九月，廣州華夏職業學院投資建設的大學生藝術旅館在蓮麻村正式動工。該項目計畫歷時三個月，總投資六百萬元，通過盤活閒置農舍打造現代和生態特色合一的藝術基地，促進當地農村經濟發展。

　　藝術旅館工地不遠處，民宿建設正火熱進行。在村委旁邊，一家名叫「嵐塢」的民宿尤其顯眼。走進這家民宿，處處充滿農家的自然氣息，漂亮而又不失鄉間樂趣。這是村民陳惠春的家改造而成的蓮麻村首家民宿。

　　自二〇一五年底試業以來，陳惠春家的民宿受到遊客歡迎。過往，陳惠春只是一名普通的農家主婦，日常在家種菜打理家務。而今，因應「蓮麻小鎮」的快速發展，她當起了「掌櫃」，獲得一份固定收入。

　　呂田鎮相關負責人表示，政府支持農戶建設民宿農家樂，首期將選擇十家作為試點，財政資金適度支持，採取「政府+村集體+農戶」的合作模式來打造。這些村民民宿農家樂都將由村集體籌建的廣州北景源旅遊開發有限公司統一規劃管理，這樣可以避免蓮麻民宿農家樂陷於無序發展和惡性競爭。

　　除了民宿，以都市農業、文化旅遊為特色的花生油土作坊、廣州美院畫家創作旅館等都在火熱建設中。其中，能接待三百名遊客的蓮麻會務中心及青年旅社將在二〇一七年完工啟用。眼下，陳惠春正和村民商議，擴大民宿的經營範圍，搶占國慶商機。「未來，將會有更多的特色文旅設施在蓮麻湧現。」她憧憬道。

與蓮麻河並行向北的古驛道留存至今只剩下三百米，村委會翻查過明清資料，按照歷史書卷隻言片語的描繪加以修繕。村支書潘光灶期望，翻新的古驛道能夠「說出」舊時的蓮麻故事。「引進項目並不意味著大拆大建，立足蓮麻傳統，原汁原味保留鄉村生態特色是『蓮麻小鎮』的建設理念。」呂田鎮相關負責人表示，早在建設之初，就專門邀請中國鄉村建設院團隊到訪，並一同打磨「蓮麻小鎮」規劃建設方案，呈現鄉村特色成為主要焦點。

「蓮麻土法豆腐和土榨花生油遠近馳名，是當地的特色農產品，引進企業以工業化的手段幫助農民升級生產力，不僅是擴大生產，更重要的是展現農村的傳統工藝。」他透露，目前，白酒作坊已邀請五糧液大師前來教學，提煉釀酒的文化價值。

從化商人羅霆近年尋求新產業的投資機遇，十多年沒有回家鄉的他在今年春節來到了蓮麻，「小鎮建設如火如荼，滿地都是機遇」。商業嗅覺靈敏的羅霆在春節決心回到家鄉，投資都市農業。

第一步是翻新農舍，邀請設計師規劃建設農家樂；第二步是發展綠色莊園，與村民合作「試水」規模種植、養殖，發展當地特色的都市農業。從傳統鋼鐵貿易轉身「掘金」現代農業的羅霆在蓮麻找到了傳統資本向新業態轉型的附著點，而藉助廣州最北得天獨厚的生態環境，越來越多像羅霆這樣的投資者把資本向蓮麻的優質生態資源靠攏。目前，蓮麻村引進了多家企業，來自流溪河源頭的綠色農產品和農家文化產品將走向珠三角。

創客進村加速「小鎮」建設

國慶假期臨近，八〇後女青年潘安娜需要在蓮麻周邊走訪，加緊準備物料，以應對國慶的人流高峰。二〇〇六年大學畢業後，潘安娜先後在鎮政府等單位就職。二〇一五年底，她選擇紮根蓮麻村，籌建她人生的第一個創業項目——「北源之家」。

「北是指廣州最北，源是流溪河源頭的意思，我們希望能給顧客家一般的溫暖。」潘安娜投資不多，她先從盤活泥磚屋起步，通過裝修和修繕，把農舍裝扮一新。

二〇一五年底經營至今，「北源之家」在互聯網上小有名氣，而通過「北源之家」的住宿和服務，遊人們對蓮麻有了更深刻的認識。潘安娜說，作為小本經營的創客，她把每月的盈利都滾動投到旅館和周邊建設，比如為小溪增加護欄，鋪設青磚，一點一點完善周邊的設施。

生態旅遊、現代農業「攪動」農村產業新脈動，綠色經濟帶來的發展機遇讓年輕人重新回流蓮麻村。「現在得知特色小鎮發展火熱，越來越多年輕人進村尋求機遇，裡面既有年輕村民，也有學生，還有一些創業人士。」潘光灶說，光是出外打工回流的本村青年就有十幾戶，人口結構的變化為這座山區農村注入新活力，小鎮建設正在提速。

任何的改革都並非一帆風順，對於蓮麻村發生的改變，村民的不理解源於不瞭解，村民的支持則源於切身感受到改變帶來的實惠。潘光灶說，蓮麻村的發展定位是打造生態旅遊景區，因此，配套建設民宿、農家樂和鄉村酒店是蓮麻村今後一個時期的重要項目之一。隨著宣傳效應帶來的影響力，蓮麻村寧靜清新的自然環境吸引了很多遊客前來一探究竟。潘光灶介紹：「目前，我村已開業的農家樂共有三家，每逢週六日或者公眾假期，到這裡來吃農家菜和住宿的遊客特別多，其中一家從春節到現在，已經獲得十萬元的收入。」二〇一六年一月份，大廣高速的開通給蓮麻村帶來了很大的影響，在村委幹部的爭取下，大廣高速地派出口增加了「蓮麻村」的字眼，這大大增加了蓮麻村的知名度。從地派出口下高速，只需要經過五公里的國道就可以抵達蓮麻村，如今，從廣州城區到蓮麻村只需要八十分鐘的車程，十分方便快捷。在二〇一六年「五一」假期，蓮麻村的農家樂入住率爆滿，供不應求。

為鼓勵村民大力支持家鄉的建設發展，提高村民的創業積極性，村委還制定了優惠政策，率先投入建設民宿、農家樂的前十戶將獲得五萬元的贊助款。目前蓮麻村正在開展的大大小小項目中，涉及人力、機械設備等資源的，在同等條件下，將會優先考慮該村村民，為他們帶來就業機會，增加村民收入。

從化特色小鎮成區域創新「新引擎」

　　二〇一六年十一月最後一個週末，廣州首屆稻草節在從化西塘村拉開帷幕。本屆稻草節主題不僅是生態旅遊和休閒觀光，更是動漫協會和西塘童話小鎮的首度「牽手」——動漫元素走進童話小鎮核心區的開始。早前，國家體育總局有關部門與從化區正式簽訂「全國戶外產業示範區」合作協議，未來五年，包括廣州露營大會、戶外運動節、全國登山健身大會等大型賽事及活動陸續落地特色小鎮。在品牌活動引領下，來自全國的人流、信息流、資金流等要素將與從化產生連接。

　　秋收後，從化鰲頭鎮西塘村遍地是金色的稻田。每年十一月底，當地人就把稻草做成簡單的稻草人供村民娛樂。二〇一六年稻草節升級成為全市規模的大型活動，為西塘村帶來龐大的人流和商機。

　　西塘村位於鰲頭鎮東北部，S355 線道旁，面積約四點二平方公里，東距從化城區十一公里，南距廣州市區六十公里，全村耕地有一千九百九十八畝。舊時的西塘村發展滯後，村裡大部分青壯年都外出務工。

　　二〇一五年底，西塘村納入從化特色小鎮建設中，並定義為「童話小鎮」。如何把童話變為現實？「首先是基礎設施建設、村容環境整治，其次是引進企業注入發展的內生動力，最後是動漫元素和資源的進駐。」鰲頭鎮有關負責人表示。

「西塘生態資源豐富，打通生態到產業的通道，為農村注入發展活力，是當地人最殷切的期望。」西塘村支書陳海濤說，二〇一六年初，西塘村先後引進三家都市型農業企業，幾個月前，陸續有村民回流尋找就業機遇，昔日冷清的農村頓時熱鬧起來。三十名本地村民變身為大棚工人，他們每天需要管理好蔬菜，並按照需求匹配蔬菜到不同的家庭包裹裡，最後通過冷鏈配送到廣州兩百個家庭。

「西塘稻草節背後實際上是搭建平台打出小鎮知名度，引進更多企業，融合動漫文化發展以『三農』為核心內容的童話旅遊小鎮。」從化區有關負責人透露策劃稻草節幕後的「野心」。

西塘村二〇一六年十九個特色小鎮建設項目已全部進入實施階段。稻草節後，西塘將迎來新一輪的改造，未來還將整合資源建設「種子王國」「昆蟲王國」，為前來發展的動漫企業提供寫生及觸發靈感的生態科普地。

寶趣玫瑰世界、櫻花園、萬花園，多個生態旅遊景區，數片燦爛花海，將西和村勾勒成一幅極具風情的畫作。在特色小鎮建設項目的帶動下，政府推動退果還田和土地流轉，吸引企業落戶。西和村負責人說，當地大棚生產的高產值、高附加值的農業生產結構模式，實現了花卉生產產業化，提高了土地的種植效益。目前，西和美麗小鎮已進駐三十五家企業，已投入生產面積一萬多畝，初步形成以生產鮮切花、蘭花、盆花、櫻花、特色苗木為主體的花卉生產及觀光產業。

「西和村要打造成廣州最具風情的小鎮，建設廣東唯一的特色農業公園。」從化城郊街道相關負責人介紹。從北部呂田到溫泉再到南部城郊，幾個特色小鎮初步成型，串珠成鏈展現出不同以往的面貌。

　　目前，從化通過論證調研，已形成以露營和徒步為特色的廣州最北的蓮麻小鎮；依託花卉特色資源打造成嶺南花海於一體的西和風情小鎮；以特色金融、創業創新、婚慶浪漫為產業的溫泉財富小鎮；以童話為主題針對兒童及親子市場打造西塘童話小鎮。

到二〇二〇年廣東擬建成百個省級特色小鎮

特色小鎮是指在城鎮（城市）的特定區域，以特色產業集聚發展為特徵，融合產業、文化、旅遊、生活等功能的新型發展空間。

廣東將以特色主導產業和經典產業為重點，打造九大特色小鎮。特色小鎮要突出一個「特」字，產業有特色，特色小鎮的形態也要「特」。

同時，特色小鎮還是促進創新創業，在國內同樣推廣建設特色小鎮的浙江，特色小鎮促進有效投資、激活消費熱情的效果已然顯現。以東莞市松山湖為例，據介紹，當地正努力建設「互聯網+」小鎮，結合自身產業特點，積極完善小鎮創新創業生態，互聯網特色產業集群初具規模。到二〇一八年，小鎮將建成兩百二十萬平方米的創業基地，力爭培育三到五家互聯網產業龍頭企業、五百家互聯網創新型中小企業。

昌明文庫·悅讀中國　A0607035

中國夢·廣東故事——共享的廣東

作　　者	王　鶴	
版權策畫	李煥芹	
責任編輯	呂玉姍	
發 行 人	陳滿銘	
總 經 理	梁錦興	
總 編 輯	陳滿銘	
副總編輯	張晏瑞	
編 輯 所	萬卷樓圖書股份有限公司	
排　　版	菩薩蠻數位文化有限公司	
印　　刷	百通科技股份有限公司	
封面設計	菩薩蠻數位文化有限公司	
出　　版	昌明文化有限公司	

桃園市龜山區中原街 32 號

電話 (02)23216565

發　　行　萬卷樓圖書股份有限公司

臺北市羅斯福路二段 41 號 6 樓之 3

電話 (02)23216565

傳真 (02)23218698

電郵 SERVICE@WANJUAN.COM.TW

大陸經銷

廈門外圖臺灣書店有限公司

電郵 JKB188@188.COM

ISBN 978-986-496-397-3

2019 年 3 月初版

定價：新臺幣 300 元

如何購買本書：

1. 轉帳購書，請透過以下帳戶

合作金庫銀行 古亭分行

戶名：萬卷樓圖書股份有限公司

帳號：0877717092596

2. 網路購書，請透過萬卷樓網站

網址 WWW.WANJUAN.COM.TW

大量購書，請直接聯繫我們，將有專人為您

服務。客服：(02)23216565　分機 610

如有缺頁、破損或裝訂錯誤，請寄回更換

國家圖書館出版品預行編目資料

中國夢.廣東故事 ——共享的廣東 / 王鶴著.
-- 初版.-- 桃園市：昌明文化出版；臺北
市：萬卷樓發行, 2019.03
　冊；　 公分
ISBN 978-986-496-397-3(平裝)

1.區域研究 2.廣東省

673.3　　　　　　　　　108002847